CARREERS

Becoming a Partner

Fifth edition

Reference Use Only

Not to be removed from the library

BPP College

069815

Related titles by Law Society Publishing

Excellent Client Service
Heather Stewart
1 85328 777 6

Marketing Your Law Firm
Lucy Adam
1 85328 745 8

Marketing, Management and Motivation
Diane Bown-Wilson and Gail Courtney
1 85328 810 1

Media Relations for Lawyers
Sue Stapley
1 85328 291 X

Quality Management for Law Firms
Matthew Moore
1 85328 715 6

Setting Up and Managing a Small Practice
Martin Smith
1 85328 348 7

Solicitors' Guide to Good Management
Trevor Boutall and Bill Blackburn
1 85328 732 6

Titles from Law Society Publishing can be ordered from all good legal bookshops or direct from our distributors, Marston Book Services (telephone 01235 465656 or e-mail *law.society@ marston.co.uk*). For further information or a catalogue call our editorial and marketing office on 020 7320 5878.

Becoming a Partner

Fifth edition

youngsolicitorsgroup

The Law Society

All rights reserved. No part of this publication may be reproduced in any material form, whether by photocopying, scanning, downloading onto computer or otherwise without the written permission of the Law Society and the authors except in accordance with the provisions of the Copyright, Designs and Patents Act 1988. Applications should be addressed in the first instance, in writing, to Law Society Publishing. Any unauthorised or restricted act in relation to this publication may result in civil proceedings and/or criminal prosecution.

The authors have asserted the right under the Copyright, Designs and Patents Act 1988 to be identified as authors of this work.

© The Law Society 2003

ISBN–10: 1–85328–841–1

ISBN–13: 978–1–85328–841–8

Published in 2003 by the Law Society
113 Chancery Lane, London WC2A 1PL

Reprinted in 2005

Typeset by J&L Composition, Filey, North Yorkshire
Printed by TJ International Ltd, Padstow, Cornwall

No part of this book constitutes financial advice. Readers are encouraged to seek independent advice on matters arising from an offer of partnership. The authors and publishers cannot accept any responsibility for loss occasioned to any person acting or refraining from action as a result of the material in this publication.

Contents

Acknowledgements

The Young Solicitors Group would like to thank the following people for their hard work in writing the previous (fourth) edition: Frank Maher, Andrew Greenfield, Richard Adams, Simon Arscott, Bill Gornall-King, Sandra Graham, Anna Hall, Clive Newnham, Michael Ord, Margaret Tofalides, Lucy Winskell, Jayne Willetts and John Willis.

Thank you also to the following for their kind contributions and updating work on the fifth edition:

- Catherine Bradley (Terrence Higgins Trust) and Tony Roe (Boyes Turner);
- Tracy Calvert, Chris Bramall, Penny Butler and Judith McDermott (the Law Society) particularly Chapters 6 and 15;
- Brian Palmer (Palmer & Co) for Chapters 10–12;
- Michael Simmons (Finers Stephens Innocent) for Chapter 13;
- Ian Morrell, Bernadette Romain-Barton, Mark Hoskin, Mark Dear (Holden-Meehan Ltd) for Chapter 14;
- Tony Sacker (Kingsley Napley) for Chapter 8.

About the Young Solicitors Group

Who we are

The Young Solicitors Group (YSG) is a recognised Law Society Group run as a company limited by guarantee, representing approximately 50,000 members and associate members of the Law Society throughout England and Wales who are under the age of 36 or who are less than five years qualified. Currently, membership of YSG is free and automatic upon registration with the Law Society.

Our history

The YSG was originally founded in 1960 by a grouping of young solicitors in the London area. Since then, the group has evolved into a national organisation representing and serving the interests of over 50 per cent of the solicitors' profession in England and Wales.

What we do

On a national level, the YSG co-ordinates policy issues, participates in consultation exercises, and lobbies the Law Society, the Government and others on issues that affect the daily lives of young solicitors. We work on a daily basis with the policy makers within the Law Society, providing a young solicitor's perspective to their issues, with a view to shaping regulations and decisions before they have been made. We are helped in this task by having two dedicated seats on the Law Society's Council (the body of 105 people who run the Law Society): one seat for newly qualified solicitors and one seat for young solicitors.

The YSG also organises consultations on topics of interest to its members, and conducts research to provide the profession with necessary statistical information on problems faced by young solicitors. Finally, the YSG provides a number of key benefits for its members. In particular, every young solicitor who is registered with us receives a free copy of YSG magazine every two months, has access to a range of free or cut price CPD-rated lectures and conferences and can choose to receive free legal update e-mails every day, giving all the latest developments in their specified area(s) of legal practice.

At a local level, around 30 local YSG groups provide a range of services and benefits to the legal communities in their areas. Most major legal centres in England and Wales have a local YSG group, which organises social activities (balls, drinks evenings, etc.), sports events (football, softball, netball, etc.) and educational lectures. The local groups also help to implement the policy set by the national committee, and to feed back issues and problems faced by members in their areas. Most local YSG groups charge a small annual membership fee to cover the cost of their administration/subsidise the events arranged. Details of local groups can be found on the YSG's website (**www.ysg.org**) or by calling 020 7320 5793.

The objectives of YSG

To quote from the Memorandum and Articles of Association:

3. The objects for which the YSG is established are:

    (a) to promote and further the interests of the members of the YSG and young solicitors;

    (b) to promote the social, cultural and educational activities of members of the YSG and young solicitors;

    (c) to maintain the welfare of the members of the YSG and young solicitors;

    (d) to maintain and promote co-operation with other legal organisations;

    (e) to maintain and further good working relations between members of the YSG and young solicitors and those for whom they work;

(f)   to represent members of the YSG and young solicitors within and without the Law Society of England and Wales;

(g)   to promote the provision of pro bono legal advice, charitable support and undertaking of community activities by members of the YSG, young solicitors and those for whom they work;

(h)   to issue appeals, hold public meetings, lectures, exhibitions and entertainments and take all such other steps as may be necessary for the purpose of promoting and publicising the objects of the YSG or procuring contributions to its funds in the form of donations, subscriptions, covenants and otherwise. . .

How to get involved

The YSG and its local groups are always on the lookout for volunteers to assist with the organisation of events and preparation of policy papers. Every year, the activities of the YSG alone involve the equivalent of around £290,000 of volunteer time (at Civil Legal Aid rates). On top of this, there are many meetings and local group activities that need your support.

If you are interested in a particular issue or want to help organise a particular event that will benefit young solicitors, please contact us or your local group. If you have plenty of free time available and want to get more involved, you could seek to be appointed to the national committee of YSG as the representative of your local group. This will allow you to become more familiar with the group's operations before thinking about standing for election to a position on the executive committee.

Contact us

The YSG can be contacted at the addresses below.

Business

For queries relating to YSG business activities, member benefits (including queries relating to the magazine, website or other publications), or questions in relation to administrative matters, contact:

Linda Warminger
Business Manager, Young Solicitors Group
105 St Peter's Street
St Albans
Hertfordshire
AL1 3EJ
Tel: 01727 896088
Fax: 01727 896026
E-mail: business@ysg.org

Policy

For queries relating to YSG policies on particular issues, or queries relation to pastoral care matters, contact:

Judith McDermott
Policy Manager, Young Solicitors Group
The Law Society
114 Chancery Lane
London
WC2A 1PL
Tel: 020 7320 5793
Fax: 020 7831 0170
E-mail: policy@ysg.org
Web: **www.ysg.org**

Preface

We hope you find this guide helpful. We have tried to ensure that all the information is accurate at the time of going to press, but as much depends on individual circumstances, do not end your search for advice here. As a group of volunteers, we cannot accept any responsibility for any errors in the text.

For technical detail you should consult the standard textbooks such as *Lindley and Banks on Partnership* 18th edn (Sweet & Maxwell, 2002) and taxation manuals such as Tolley's Tax Guides. You will find the Solicitors' Practice Rules and guidance in *The Guide to the Professional Conduct of Solicitors 1999* published by the Law Society, updated at **www.guide-on-line.lawsociety.org.uk** and in *Cordery on Solicitors* 9th edn (Butterworths, 1996).

We hope to give you the benefit of our practical experience and highlighted areas of concern. Particularly important aspects may be repeated partially in different chapters and this is deliberate for emphasis and to make each chapter more or less self-contained.

We have tried to cover as many aspects of partnership as possible, but inevitably we will not have covered every situation. We welcome any practical suggestions you may have for later editions of this work. Please send these to the YSG Policy Manager at the Law Society.

Foreword

This guide is the fifth edition of a book written by the Young Solicitors Group (YSG); the fourth edition was published by the Law Society in 1992 and previous editions were known as *Partnership Problems and Pitfalls*. The aim of the guide has remained the same over many years and editions – to provide practical assistance to young solicitors considering partnership. We hope this edition more accurately reflects the changing legal landscape.

Complex issues face young solicitors considering partnership. For example, in small firms, partnership may be offered prematurely as a way of raising revenue and spreading risk. Also, cuts to the legal aid system have placed many firms under extreme financial pressure, which a young solicitor being offered partnership may not be fully aware of when considering this important career decision.

Many young solicitors face personal financial pressure as the legacy of university and law school loans and must consider all the issues carefully before exposing themselves to further potential financial risk by entering a partnership.

Expectations of a healthy work/life balance have also changed in the last 10 years. More and more young solicitors are assessing whether or not they are prepared to commit to the long hours culture traditionally associated with partnership in private practice.

As with previous editions, we have tried to keep this guide practical and non-technical. It is not a substitute for obtaining proper professional advice, nor is it intended to recommend partnership as the 'holy grail'. We hope that it will assist young solicitors who may be considering a number of career progression options and help them to identify whether or not partnership is in fact for them.

Partnership can be a most rewarding career choice and we hope that this guide will help the reader reach an informed decision and negotiate a partnership deed that meets his or her needs and fulfils expectations, thus ensuring a rewarding and secure future in the profession.

In many ways a partnership is like a marriage; there must be trust, co-operation and candour between the parties. Before making what is potentially a life-long commitment to a firm, it is vital to ensure that you really do subscribe to the firm's ethos. For example, does the firm contribute to the local community by way of pro bono projects? Are the employees supported and encouraged to develop existing skills and learn new ones? Is staff retention an issue?

Most young solicitors want more from their firm than a salary at the end of the month. They want to work in a challenging professional environment where high standards in all areas prevail. We hope this guide will assist you in knowing the questions to ask to ensure that the firm is right for you.

Mary-Ann Wright
Chair, Young Solicitors Group 2001–2002

Deciding whether to become a partner

Introduction

The idea of partnership is essentially one of a long-term relationship and you should assess any offer of partnership with that in mind. When you receive an invitation to become a partner, it may well evoke similar feelings to those of a marriage proposal. You should, therefore, first of all consider whether you will be able to get on with the existing partners and whether they will be able to get on with you – although they would not be making an offer to you without having considered this.

A good starting point is if there's a general agreement in underlying philosophies between the existing partners and you. You cannot expect to agree with all your partners all the time, indeed such a state of affairs is unlikely in a healthy partnership. However, if you and your partners are completely at odds then there will be disagreements – perhaps of a very substantial nature – in the future. You should therefore consider your prospective partners carefully.

The next step is to consider what your ambitions are, both personally and professionally. Are you going to achieve these within the firm, given the nature of the work undertaken, and the general working environment? In short, are you likely to obtain job satisfaction as a partner within the firm? Equally, do you hope to specialise in any particular area of law in the future and will the firm and its structure give you a realistic opportunity to fulfil that wish?

Practical considerations

You should consider very carefully the change in status that follows becoming a partner. You will cease to be an employee, and become an employer. This means first of all a loss of rights, and secondly an acceptance of liability. The shift from employed to self-employed status means you immediately lose the statutory protection that you had against unfair dismissal in relation to redundancy. If you are a woman, you lose your maternity rights. As a self-employed individual certain state benefits are no longer available to you, although there is a financial benefit, for example in reduced payments of national insurance contributions.

In addition, as a partner, you accept unlimited liability for the debts and obligations of the firm, unless it is a limited liability partnership. While this liability is joint and several as between you and your partners, you should remember that any further creditor of the firm may seek redress from any or all of the partners even after the partnership has been dissolved or you have left. Further, your liability is not only for normal trading debts such as suppliers' bills but also for any other wrong including negligence, misappropriation or loss of property or funds, or, for example, if a defamatory letter is written on the firm's notepaper. You also become personally liable for ensuring that the firm complies with the relevant Solicitors' Practice Rules.

You may be offered a partnership either wholly or partially salaried, but in any event you should remember that partners can only take out profits from a firm if profits are made; in accepting partnership you are losing the security of a wage. You are putting your faith in the ability of the partnership to make money.

Financial and personal commitments

As a partner you are making a commitment on both a personal level and financial level to your firm and your partners. On a personal level, as a partner you assume (jointly and severally with your partners) all the responsibilities of managing the firm, the duties (statutory and otherwise with civil and criminal sanctions) which fall on all employers, and the requirement to earn fees and make profits for the firm. While some or all of the managerial or administrative responsibilities may well be delegated to one or more partners or, for example, to a partnership secretary, the duty to ensure that these responsibilities are met still rests with you and your partners.

On a financial level you may be asked to make a capital contribution to the firm, in effect to purchase shares within the firm which entitle you to a proportion of the profits, or to buy a share in the fixed assets or goodwill of the firm. Some firms have arrangements in place so that partners can borrow against goodwill or pay in instalments out of profits. It may be that you will be expected to leave profits in the firm over a period of time to make up such a contribution, but possibly you will be asked to make a significant immediate payment on becoming a partner. It is more than likely that if you have to make such a contribution, you will incur personal borrowings. You have to consider the cost of financing such a loan when you are assessing the financial benefits likely to accrue from becoming a partner. You should also remember that a loan incurred for the purpose of buying into a partnership will generally qualify for tax relief on interest repayment.

Essential information

As a prospective or incoming partner the strength of your bargaining position in any negotiations which you have with the firm may vary and the existing partners will of course protect their own legitimate interests. There are documents and other information, which you should study before making a decision as to whether or not to accept an offer of partnership.

You should first look at the firm's accounts (see Chapter 10). As a general rule you should note the trends which the accounts disclose and judge the firm's future accordingly. Of course if you have worked for the firm for some time, you will be familiar with a number of the firm's strengths and weaknesses. It is vital that you are realistic in assessing these. Some of the existing partners may be reluctant to disclose copies of the accounts. However, if you are to take on the responsibilities for the firm's liabilities and especially if you are contemplating a significant capital contribution, then you must have an opportunity to study the accounts and the firm's financial position.

You also need to examine the partnership agreement or deed itself. In particular you should look closely at the arrangements for:

- bringing in new partners;
- allowing partners to retire;
- the age at which partners are compelled to leave the firm;
- making capital contributions;

- profit sharing;
- re-distributing or re-assessing profit shares in the future; and
- dismissing a partner.

You should study any restrictive covenants that you are being asked to sign. You should take the opportunity to consider whether there are any appropriate amendments which could be made to the partnership deed and propose them to existing partners.

You will need to clarify the precise terms that the partners are offering. This may sound obvious, but many offers to join a partnership are at best general, and at worst vague. You should find out exactly what you are being offered and what your partners are, in turn, expecting of you. If you are being offered a salaried partnership, you should find out whether that is to be for a definite or indefinite period, and what terms, if any, are in place to enable you to progress to an equity partnership. You should seek and obtain a full indemnity from the profit-sharing partners for the liabilities of the firm while you remain a salaried partner. You should bear in mind, however, that this indemnity is only worth as much as your partners themselves are worth.

You should consider the age structure of the firm, whether any age group is dominant within the partnership or whether there are any gaps in the age structure. If the latter, and such a gap is in a key department within the firm, you might consider whether this is likely to pose a credibility problem with important clients. If some partners are approaching retirement age, or will in due course approach retirement age around the same time, consider the likely financial calls that will be made on the firm and on you when those partners retire.

Advantages and disadvantages

The disadvantages of becoming a partner can effectively be summed up in three words – assumption of risk.

As a partner in a firm you assume the risks attached to the business, and these risks can arise from all quarters:

- every management decision;
- internal disputes;

- unproductive senior partners and aggressive younger partners;
- a downturn in trade and poor profits.

There are many advantages. First and most obviously, you hope there will be financial gain, and that the combined efforts of the partners will produce profits, which will enable you as a partner to enjoy income well in excess of any salary which you would have enjoyed as an employed solicitor. In addition, as a partner you will have a say in, and an element of control over, the firm's future and your own.

In the right firm, with the appropriate level of commitment from partners and staff, the risk can be minimised and the advantages realised.

Seeking advice

In the final analysis, it is you and you alone who makes the decision about whether or not to join the firm as a partner. However, you should not take any decision about accepting, rejecting, or negotiating any offer of partnership without proper financial advice. In the first instance you should consider discussing the terms of any offer, and in particular the contents of the partnership deed, with another solicitor. You might consider it appropriate to speak to someone whom you have known for some time, whose views you trust, and who perhaps is not within the immediate geographical area of the firm you are joining. It is best to consult someone who is already a partner, because they will have gone through the same procedure and will be able to give you the benefit of their own experience and the advice they received. That same person might also be able to advise you on how to interpret the firm's accounts. However, if you are in any doubt, you should consider instructing a solicitor and/or an accountant on a professional basis to advise you. This will, of course, mean that you are incurring fees but there should be more than enough at stake to make it worthwhile incurring those charges.

Partnership checklists

If you are thinking of partnership, here are some questions you will need to ask about the business and the agreement.

CHECKLIST 1.   **The firm**

- What is the firm's business?
- When did it start?
- What majority is required to change the business?
- What is the name?
- Does the stationery contain the required information – name and partners?
- Is the name trademarked?
- Where will the firm carry out its business?

CHECKLIST 2.   **The partnership**

- How many partners?
- Is there a restriction on numbers?
- Are all the partners appropriately qualified?
- When does the partnership take effect?
- Is there a fixed term for duration?
- Is it clear that death, retirement, bankruptcy will not lead to the end of the partnership?
- Is it clear what majority can lead to the end of the partnership?
- Does anyone have a leading role?

CHECKLIST 3. **Property and goodwill**

- What are the partnership assets?
- How are they valued?
- Who owns the premises?
- If the partnership does not own the premises, what are the terms of the lease, including rent?
- How is any interest in land held?
- Who owns the goodwill?
- Are there any other assets?

CHECKLIST 4. **Partnership capital**

- In what shares is capital owned?
- How much capital is required?
- How is capital to be contributed?
- Does any partner receive interest on capital?
- Are partners charged interest on capital which has not been provided?
- What happens to capital on the death of a partner?
- How is further capital to be raised and how is this decided?
- What is the relationship between capital ratios and profit sharing ratios?
- How does revaluation of assets affect capital shares?

CHECKLIST 5. **Finances**

- How does the firm calculate profits and losses?
- How are profits and losses shared?
- Are there profit-related bonuses and how are they distributed?

- Are there any related financial benefits?
- How is work in progress valued?
- What is the bank balance?
- What is the ratio of partners' capital to borrowings?
- What are the liabilities?
- Are partners expected to account for external income?
- Are there future plans for expansion?
- How much can each partner draw and when?
- What controls are there on partner drawings?
- How are partners' tax liabilities dealt with?
- Who keeps the accounts?
- How accessible are the accounts?
- Do the accounts include goodwill?
- How are the accounts agreed?
- Have the accounts been filed in a timely way and are they up to date?
- Who has authority to sign cheques and for how much?
- How many partners sign cheques?
- What financial controls and checks are there on client accounts?

CHECKLIST 6. **Insurance**

- What policies are in place – professional indemnity insurance, public liability insurance, employers' liability insurance, public liability insurance, property insurance, car insurance, health insurance, loss of profits arising from damage to equipment including computers?
- Are other policies needed?
- What is the claims record?
- What is the deductible/excess?

CHECKLIST 7.   **Management and duties**

- Are the partners' roles clearly defined?
- Is it clear that partners have to achieve agreed targets/goals?
- Is there any flexibility on the type of work partners can undertake?
- What majority is required for taking decisions?
- Are management decisions delegated?
- Who is responsible for financial decisions and accountability?
- How are partnership meetings held?
- Are there arrangements for proxy voting?
- What happens when a partner is sick?

CHECKLIST 8.   **Incoming partners**

- How are they to be appointed?
- How much capital do they contribute?
- How are profits shared?
- How are salaried partners appointed?

CHECKLIST 9.   **Leaving the partnership**

- Can partners be expelled/suspended and what majority is required?
- At what age does a partner retire?
- Is there provision for early retirement?
- Do retired partners continue as consultants?
- Can a partner be excluded from the offices?
- What are the financial arrangements on retirement?
- Is capital repaid to outgoing partners in instalments?

- How is capital repaid?
- Is capital re-valued on departure of a partner?
- What happens to profits?
- What happens to property belonging to an outgoing partner?
- Is there any indemnity to outgoing partners in respect of debts or future liabilities?
- Are there restrictive covenants?
- Is there a restriction on taking clients?
- Are partners prevented from undertaking certain kinds of work and for how long and within what geographical limits?
- How are partnership debts repaid?

CHECKLIST 10.   **Changing or ending the partnership**

- What partnership majority is needed to change the partnership?
- Does the agreement prevent dissolution on expulsion, death or bankruptcy of a partner?
- Does the partnership end after a fixed term?
- Can an individual partner dissolve the firm?
- How are partnership assets treated on dissolution?
- How is profit to be distributed?

CHECKLIST 11. **Other**

- Can any disputes be resolved by alternative means?
- What are the provisions for holidays, sick leave, sabbatical, maternity, compassionate leave?
- What provisions are there for incapacity?
- Are medical checks required?
- Who pays for partners' health and life insurance?
- What provisions are made for partners' savings?
- What are the arrangements for pensions?

Assessing the firm

Offers from your own firm

In most cases you are asked to join the partnership where you have been employed as an assistant solicitor. You will therefore have some knowledge of the way in which the partnership functions and will have formed a view of the personalities of the respective partners themselves.

When you are asked to become a partner of your existing firm, you will already be familiar with partnership politics. Obviously, there are different considerations depending on the type of firm. In a large city firm it is almost impossible to know all the partners. Indeed, in some cases it may be difficult to know all the partners within your own department. You will have to decide whether you can be happy in that environment. It suits some but not others. Some people are more than happy to work with partners with whom they do not particularly want to socialise, but whom they trust and respect within the working environment. In smaller firms one of the considerations is that you will have to work closely with a few individuals and you need to know that communications will not break down because you are out of sympathy. There is nothing more difficult than trying to work with someone who has lost your respect.

Offers from other firms

You may be approached by another firm to join them as a partner. This may be a firm with which you have had successful dealings in the course of your work, or perhaps a firm with which you have social contacts. This firm may be attracted by your client base, which they hope will follow you, or you may have expertise in a particular field which they are lacking.

In either case, you should be cautious. It is fine to have successful dealings with others who have been professional, efficient and friendly in their manner. There is, however, a world of difference between enjoying a game of squash with or doing the same gym class as fellow solicitors, or moving in the same social circle, and working together. You should be cautious because solicitors who are socially charming may not be the easiest people with whom to work. Some have irritating idiosyncrasies and others may be completely intolerable in the office!

If you are in a situation that involves moving to a new firm and you have no experience of working with your new colleagues, you may be advised to join the new firm as an associate for a limited period, perhaps six months, and then at the end of that time join the partnership. This has benefits for both the existing partners and you, in that it allows a little time for 'teething problems' to be sorted out, and for you to be absolutely satisfied that you have confidence in your new colleagues. Similarly, the existing partnership will be absolutely sure that their new partner is of the calibre they seek.

Trust

The golden rule, and this is as relevant for a large firm as a two-partner firm, is that if you cannot trust your partners you should not join the partnership. Trust is not just about financial issues, in other words will the partners mishandle or misappropriate funds, but also other factors such as presenting the correct image of the partnership to other solicitors, clients and potential clients. If you do not trust your partners to be efficient or businesslike or entirely truthful, then others are likely to have the same perception. Remember that your partners' actions may affect you and your livelihood and may well impact on outsiders' perceptions of you.

Something you must consider, and particularly in a smaller firm, is the amount of work you will be expected to do. Some small partnerships work with one partner doing all the work, putting in long hours even coming into the office at weekends, whereas the other seems to spend more time out of the office than in! If that partner is cultivating potential clients and bringing in the work, this may not be a problem. However, if this imbalance is going to lead to resentment, you should head it off as soon as possible. In this situation you might have to think hard about the profit-sharing arrangements.

If you are not happy with the general feel of the firm, you should take steps to discuss this with your partners as soon as possible, and look for an early remedy. For example, you may feel that some of your partners are overcharging clients, which may act to the detriment of the firm as a whole because they could be losing clients in the long term. Address such issues early to avoid conflict.

Profit-sharing arrangements

No two firms of solicitors are the same, and there is no universal formula in relation to profit sharing. However, when you are invited to join the partnership this is clearly something you have to consider carefully. As a general rule, the partnership should review profit sharing annually. Not only does this give you an opportunity to weigh up whether there should be variations to the policy, but you can then gain a general view of the partnership. It is essential that all parties' interests are taken into consideration when reviewing the profit-sharing policy. This will depend on the size of the firm.

Some larger firms prefer to have a very structured scheme with an equity points system of profit sharing, whereby the profit share is adjusted at regular intervals by varying the number of points in a scale, the number of years to parity, and the rate of progression to parity. Others have developed schemes which take into account not only the points raised above, but other important considerations, such as the management and administrative role played by the partner, their ability to bring work into the firm and their general role in the partnership whether or not that is dependent on their fee-earning.

In smaller firms it is likely to be obvious who is taking the greater burden of responsibility for running the firm and bringing in profits. This should make negotiations simpler and fairer. An element of flexibility has to be allowed to reflect changing circumstances. Some of the larger firms have experienced problems over profit sharing, and have noticed a resentment building up between senior partners, whose profit shares are greater, and the rather more progressive and higher fee-earning junior partners. For these reasons it may be advantageous for you and your partners to have an automatic procedure for altering the profit sharing annually as this avoids an annual round of negotiation.

Having a say in the partnership

Occasionally a somewhat dictatorial senior partner will run a firm extremely effectively, however partnerships should generally avoid this situation. A partnership is, after all, just that – an opportunity to work with others who think more or less the same way as you do about the law and about running a business. Clearly, some partners will be experts in particular fields – one might, for example, have excellent personal skills and be a good manager of the staff and therefore be put in charge of personnel. Nevertheless, you may have something to contribute in an area that is regarded as someone else's speciality.

There should be regular partners' meetings, at least bi-monthly. These should be conducted in such a way that partners can make their contribution to the running of the firm. In larger firms there should perhaps be monthly meetings of an executive partnership committee and there should be some flexibility and rotation of partners on that committee to make sure that all interests of the partners are properly represented and everybody has a voice. After all the interests of those partners approaching retirement may be very different from the incoming partners.

In smaller firms it may be possible to have your say more easily, but even then it may be easier to leave all the substantive decisions to one individual leaving the other partners to do the work.

The claims record and deductible

Of course even solicitors occasionally make mistakes. What happens if a client sues the partnership? As a partner you are liable for the losses (as well as qualifying for the profits) of a partnership. You should consider the insurance position (see Chapters 14 and 15).

All partners should be covered for professional indemnity by an insurance policy, which partners have to pay for. Insurance provides cover for claims brought against the firm including negligence, breach of contract, defamation, and breach of undertaking, but not death or personal injury or damage to property, breach of the partnership agreement, non-payment of a trading debt, wrongful dismissal or termination of employment.

Regardless of the size of the firm you are joining, you should investigate the claims record of the firm. In particular, you should be aware of the number of claims and size of claims made by the firm over the last five years and the number of outstanding claims. If you are refused this information, not only should you be suspicious, but you should also ask for a breakdown of the premiums paid by the firm, at the very least. You should attempt to ensure that any errors or claims made prior to you joining the partnership are not your responsibility. It is not unreasonable to request an indemnity for these.

You should also be aware of limitations on the policy. There is an indemnity limit for each and every claim; you should enquire about the level of cover. This 'top-up' cover may have more conditions placed on it, and be banded as the cover increases. Conditions imposed may exclude liability for the dishonesty of a partner or for US claims.

Insurance premiums will depend on the size of the practice, its location, the type of work (criminal law and the collection of judgment debts are regarded as low-risk work), and the practice's claims record. Firms may spread the loading between departments or partners. Are you entering a high-risk area?

Any payment of damages or claimant's costs will involve payment of an excess or 'deductible'; the amount will vary from firm to firm. You should check the current position with the existing partners. Check whether the partnership has increased or decreased the amount deductible by paying a smaller or greater premium. It is worth checking the partnership deed to discover who pays the deductible. It is possible that partners may be expected to pay for their own mistakes. Ordinarily, the deductible is paid as a partnership expense before division. This may affect your profit share. Once you have found out what sort of claims record the firm has and who pays the deductible, it is up to you to decide whether the risk is an acceptable one. You may also wish to evaluate the system used by the firm for reporting and dealing with claims: poor or slow reporting can result in loss of cover. You should also check whether there is a potential liability which is uninsured.

The client base

There are several important considerations that can only really be answered by you:

- Do you think that the firm can survive in a recession?
- Will the firm maximise profits during a boom?
- Does the firm rely on too few clients? Does the area or department in which you wish to become a partner have a strong client base?
- Will you be dependent upon other departments or partners retaining their clients?
- How financially secure are your clients?
- How much will you and your firm rely on publicly funded work, personal injury or conveyancing and will that be sufficient or economic in a few years' time?
- Does the firm rely too heavily on one area of work for its profits?
- Are there any signs a major client is dissatisfied?
- What is the firm's record of dealing with clients' complaints?

The answers to these questions will vary from firm to firm, depending on size and whether or not it is a specialist in a particular area. It is important to bear in mind the vagaries of the economy, and your clients' and your partners' strengths and weaknesses. Could your firm survive without its major client? Is any one client in a position to dictate unfairly, terms and conditions of his, her or its retainer? Some firms and departments, or even partners, have chosen to have a deliberately narrow client base. Presumably as an expert in that specialty before becoming a partner, you should be in a position to evaluate the wisdom of that decision.

It is often difficult to predict the future of the legal marketplace. These questions and answers will not be the most important ones but they may have a bearing on your overall decision:

- Is the firm expanding and taking on new work?
- Do you think that it is the right sort of work to integrate with the firm's client base?
- Is sufficient work being done to market the particular strengths of the firm?
- Is there a danger of the partnership folding if one partner were to leave with his or her clients?

Areas of practice

There are further questions to be considered:

- If the firm is split into departments, are there too many partners in the department you are being asked to join?
- Will the number of partners hinder your promotion within the partnership, and does that bother you?
- Will you be able to add to your particular expertise? Will you be forced to?
- Will you feel frustrated as partners in less congested departments progress more quickly?
- Will the concentration of partners in a particular area affect your profit share?

Of course each of the firm's partners will have their own clients and client contacts. If you specialise within a particular area, and do not have the major client or client contact, you may be in danger of losing work, if the client or the partner concerned were to leave the practice.

You may wish to keep your options open and leave for a new firm in the future. Would you be able to start a new department and bring work to another practice and would that be important to you? The firm's restrictive covenants would cover this possibility and may not be helpful. However it might offer protection should another partner leave. You should be aware of the advantages and disadvantages of working with a group of practitioners with a similar expertise, or of working on your own. Do you need colleagues to turn to, or do you like pioneering new ground?

Future planning

In the attempt to deal with the short-term problems, it is often easy for practices to overlook their long-term objectives. To this end, it is important to ensure the firm you are joining as a partner has an eye on the future, and has in place strategies and measures that will allow it to develop and thrive. If not, you could be joining a firm with a very limited horizon and a short life expectancy. It is important that firms of whatever size address their future, whether it be preservation of what they have or planning for growth and development.

You can discover whether the firm you are considering joining is actively addressing its future by simply asking the following questions:

- Does the firm have a business plan or strategy document?
- At what stage is the marketing plan?

It is important to find out not only whether the firm has a business plan identifying its objectives (say over the next three to five years) but also whether it is operating a marketing plan setting out how it is going to achieve those objectives. Depending on the size of the firm this may be particularly sophisticated, following reports prepared by professional consultants, or it may simply have been a question of the partners sitting down and establishing where the firm is now, where they want to be in the future and plotting out a route to achieve this.

Administration and staff management

It is often said that the greatest asset of any firm is its people, and this statement holds good in the legal profession. In order for a firm to operate effectively, its administration and staff management must be effective. A good working environment is vitally important to keep staff happy and achieve the best results. It is important to have clearly defined administrative roles so that everyone is aware of their responsibilities and time is not wasted by individuals undertaking roles outside their areas of responsibility. The tasks may be allocated to committees or individual partners. Functions such as the supervision and running of the accounts department, credit control, premises and office equipment are often delegated. It is important to find out about systems for reporting and who has ultimate control over delegated tasks.

As regards personnel management, in larger firms there is often a human resources manager, in other firms a particular partner may take on that role. Aside from recruitment it is vital that the human resources manager ensures that the existing staff are properly managed. This involves both dealing with problems or difficulties as they arise and in encouraging staff to perform to the best of their abilities. As in any business venture, the firm needs a human resources policy and procedures in place. Effective personnel management can ensure that a firm achieves a good level of competence in the staff and creates the best environment for stimulating and encouraging performance.

Training

In preserving and enhancing the firm's 'people asset' it is important to ensure good systems for training. The firm can implement general policies for client care and office procedures through training programmes across the board for all staff so that a consistent approach is adopted giving an identity and image to the firm. Using an appraisal system should ensure that this is monitored. The firm should make staff aware of what is expected of them and in what areas they can improve their performance and what training is on offer.

In particular, to make full use of secretarial support, training courses on the use of word processing and databases should be provided, so that information technology can increase productivity. Staff will then be properly trained enabling them to use the equipment provided effectively, ultimately leading to a higher standard of work.

Large city firms have introduced training programmes for their professional staff. It is a Law Society requirement that professional staff keep up to date on developments in the law and are able to broaden their knowledge by learning about other areas of work, which may complement the subjects with which they deal. Whatever the size of firm it is important that there is an opportunity to undergo training. Often this is concentrated at the trainee stage and trainee solicitor programmes are developed. The introduction of in-house lectures, often delivered by members of the firm, is a useful way of training professional staff throughout the firm.

All practitioners should participate in refresher training, since it will be necessary for a number of members of the firm to comply with the continuing education requirements of the Law Society (the annual requirement is 16 hours continuous professional development (CPD)). A formal programme which comprises both internal training (for which accreditation can be obtained from the Society) as well as outside training course attendance needs to be in place, which will be both cost effective to the firm and beneficial in terms of learning. Firms' liaison with local YSGs which run accredited lectures is also important in enabling a broad range of training to be attained by fee earners. Many practices also introduce computer training for fee earners and word processing courses and language classes, which can be of great value and are certainly something to be looked at for the future in any size practice.

Maternity, paternity and sabbaticals

It is important to see the provisions that firms make in all these areas. The provision for maternity/parental leave outside the statutory requirements is essential in considering partnership, not only if you are a woman but generally as a matter of good policy. The statutory provisions only apply to employees and will not apply to equity partners. In examining the partnership deed you should look for provisions for payment of remuneration in addition to the employee's statutory benefit. You should aim for something approaching full profit share, with reduced terms being negotiated for extended periods of absence although there may be a limit on the number of times this can be claimed. This very much depends on the firm's size and character and there is no norm. Often these provisions may be negotiated on an individual basis but it is important that the firm has a consistent policy. The need for adequate provision in partnership deeds to cover such arrangements is important for both present and prospective partners. Paternity leave is generally restricted to a few weeks and a firm's approach may be indicative of what they expect from their staff.

As regards sabbaticals, some firms have introduced them to improve the quality of life for partners who have been in partnership for a number of years. This may take the form of an agreement that after a specific length of time a partner may take a break of several months on full salary or drawings to pursue other activities. In some instances practices have introduced this as a compulsory requirement in the belief that it will refresh the individual and be beneficial to the practice in the long term. In all cases, it is important to ensure that when the partners are away from the practice, adequate provisions are made for work cover and client care.

Information technology

The level of technology which different firms employ will often depend on the firm's size. The use of word processing is now commonplace, as is the use of computers for e-mail, diaries, accounts, time-recording systems and websites. Firms have to ensure that they are adopting technology which is both cost-effective and increases efficiency. Staff using computers can perform many administrative functions and it is important that the firm has considered how their current software and hardware systems can be developed to enhance the firm's operational capacities.

Many firms have systems allowing fee earners to use e-mail and internet research facilities, and some larger firms may have an intranet or knowledge management system. It is important to identify the firm's needs for this sort of facility.

International perspectives

Finally, as well as considering which areas of law the practice is developing or wishes to develop, the international perspective is vitally important to future growth and development. Often international developments may be client led, where existing clients wish to expand their businesses into other jurisdictions. Sometimes international expansion may be marketing led, where practices see an opportunity to compete in another jurisdiction for the provision of legal services where there are no existing clients. It is important to ensure that the firm you are looking at has an eye for the future and has an international angle or the ability to create one when required.

The City of London has traditionally been an international centre for business and legal firms have a history of international contacts arising from this. Many legal firms, particularly larger practices have, either by necessity or design, developed their international practices by opening branch offices in other countries, or entering into joint ventures or strategic alliances with law firms in other jurisdictions. It is necessary to see whether your firm has the ability to develop international contacts and to examine what existing legal contacts it already has in other jurisdictions. Increasingly, larger provincial firms are expanding overseas work. It may be that one or two existing clients have contracts in other European countries or the US and the firm has used the services of lawyers in those jurisdictions. This has then built up a relationship between the foreign law firm and the local practice, which may be formalised in the future. Many firms have opened up offices in conjunction with foreign practices in a third jurisdiction such as Brussels, for example, where they have identified a need for a presence.

Clearly, the level of sophistication of international practice development will depend on the firm's size and the nature of the practice. However, it is important that the potential exists, if it is not already there, to serve clients' needs in other jurisdictions to the same level that you would wish them to be serviced yourself. In this way, a network of international practice can be developed as required.

A number of UK firms have joined international clubs of lawyers from other jurisdictions, forming loose federations. Having an established relationship with members of a club can facilitate obtaining advice from various locations and the use of local offices to act as a base or contact in a country when members of a firm are visiting. However, you should bear in mind relationships are not normally particularly close and are often exclusive and therefore the federations can be too large or unwieldy for the particular purpose which a practice has identified.

The firm may have embarked on joint ventures with law firms in other jurisdictions, on the basis that this is less expensive than opening a firm's own office and can help field the local market by having local lawyers in the office. The cost factor involved in opening an overseas office or entering a joint venture is high and clearly you would have to consider very carefully whether it was appropriate to take on a major financial obligation or, if the firm had already entered into one, its continuing viability. Even if firms do not readily identify the need to expand to establish international contacts or practice, it is important for the firm to identify potential international development and to see if and how contacts may develop until a firm policy is in place for the future.

Salaried partnership

Partnership, particularly in large and growing practices means many different things. Gone are the days when you were either an equity partner or an assistant solicitor. There are now many variations on the theme of partnership. This chapter discusses salaried partnership whilst Chapters 4–7 provide information on the other options.

Another choice

The most common variation is a salaried partner, sometimes called a non-equity or associate partner. To the outside world, there is no difference between an equity and salaried partner. A salaried partner is held out as a partner, as their name appears on the firm's stationery alongside the names of the equity partners. Salaried partners may be (but are not always) allowed to sign cheques on both office and client accounts in exactly the same manner as the equity partners. Salaried partners are usually entitled to attend and speak freely at partners' meetings. Practice varies from firm to firm on voting rights for salaried partners but you should be allowed to speak and may be entitled to vote on all issues except the profit-share allocation to equity partners. However, it must be appreciated that some firms place more restrictions on salaried partners' voting rights.

There are more pronounced differences in the financial position. You should ascertain whether a salaried partner in your firm is treated by the Inland Revenue as an employee under Schedule E or as self-employed under Schedule D. If treated as an employee, the salaried partner is paid a salary through PAYE. If treated as self-employed, the salaried partner is paid a share of the profits but this is limited to a fixed sum. Even if the salaried partner in your practice has traditionally been treated by the Revenue as an employee for tax purposes, you should make enquiries as it may be possible to change to self-employed status, which may be more tax efficient. You should note it is exceptional in practice for this to be allowed (tax matters are covered in more detail in Chapter 11). A salaried partner is not usually expected to contribute capital to the firm. Therefore it can be an easier financial transition from your assistant solicitor salary. Benefits in kind such as cars and private health insurance may be similar to those for equity partners. However, pensions vary from firm to firm and arrangements for a salaried partner are different from those of an equity partner (pensions are dealt with in more detail in Chapter 14).

A career path to equity partnership

A salaried partnership should be viewed as a useful stepping stone to equity partnership. Some firms require salaried partners to achieve a certain fee level before they are invited to become an equity partner. Other firms require two years' service or some other specified period as a salaried partner before equity partnership. Do not regard your time as a salaried partner as a chance for the other partners to see whether you are up to full partnership – although of course it does have this purpose. Be more positive – it enables you to judge the calibre of your partners as business managers without being fully financially committed to the partnership. You can determine from the inside whether this is the partnership for you. You should gain as much information as possible during your time as a salaried partner so that you are fully informed when the offer of equity partnership comes up. After all, if you have any doubts, it is much easier to extricate yourself from a salaried partnership than an equity partnership.

Fixed-share equity partnership

This is really another variant and is designed to ensure that the Inland Revenue is more likely to treat these type of partners as self-employed rather than employees. What would otherwise have been the monthly pay of a salaried partner is treated as a fixed share of the profits before the equity partners share the rest. The fixed-share equity partner may be expected to inject capital, perhaps provided by way of a loan with the interest paid by the firm. This fixed-share arrangement may be instead of, or as a progression from, salaried partnership.

Know your firm

Different firms have different practices on disclosure of information to prospective partners whether equity or salaried. You should always ask to see the accounts. Anyone asked to join a firm with the possibility of being jointly and severally liable for its debts within the next few years is entitled to enquire as to its financial viability. A financial commitment is likely in the near future and the immediate commitment is time and effort so financial information is therefore essential.

You need to know:

- Whether the firm has any assets, whether it owns its own office premises.
- Whether it operates a service company and if it does, for what purpose.
- How much is the overdraft?
- What is the turnover?
- What is the value of the partners' accounts?
- How are the equity partners' profit shares divided?

These points are covered in more detail in Chapter 10.

You also need to know whether you are guaranteed an equity partnership after a period agreed in advance – be wary of the eternal non-equity partnership (discussed in more detail later in this chapter).

The terms of the agreement or deed

Agreements can be executed as deeds to give effect to clauses including equity partner indemnity, indemnity as to private debts, property indemnity, trusts of property, removal of property trustee and grant of power of attorney. A debt owed under partnership becomes a specialty debt if there is a deed and will become time barred after 12 years rather than the normal six years. For more detail on partnership agreements see Chapter 8.

Terms vary considerably from firm to firm but generally speaking you can expect them to include the usual details such as duties, salary, holidays, sick pay, notice period but more importantly, the extent to which you are entitled to take part in the control and management of the firm. If you are to be a self-employed partner, the deed is likely to contain a 'guaranteed' profit share. It should outline the equity partners' responsibilities in managing the firm and whether the equity partners are obliged to account to the salaried partner about management of the firm. The deed is likely to include provisions dealing with confidentiality and with restrictive covenants; these need to be checked carefully to ensure that they are not too onerous. It is also important to insist on an arbitration clause as this is the most suitable way to deal with partnership disputes. It is best to have a named arbitrator in the agreement. The deed may also include the route by which you are to become an equity partner and what rights you have to see the accounts of the firm. An indemnity in respect of the firm's debts for which you are liable through holding out as a partner is essential and is dealt with in more detail below.

Indemnities against liabilities

The disadvantage of being a salaried partner is that you are liable for the firm's debts and obligations because you are held out as a partner to the public by appearing on the firm's stationery. However, this is theoretically counteracted by the indemnity from the other partners upon which you are entitled to insist.

If you remember nothing else from this section on salaried partnership, you should remember to obtain an indemnity from the equity partners.

This indemnity is a simple agreement between the equity partners and the salaried partners whereby the equity partners agree to indemnify the salaried partners against all debts, liabilities and obligations of the partnership. It is often drafted to exclude liabilities arising from the salaried partner's actions. It should be noted during the 1990s ex-partners found themselves being sued on leases signed many years before. In the absence of an express term indemnifying a salaried partner in respect of claims for rent, property taxes, costs of repairs and alterations, etc. it may be difficult to avoid liability on old leases. Apart from a separate deed, indemnities can also be dealt with by way of a clause in the service agreement or partnership deed.

The harsh financial reality means the importance of an indemnity cannot be too strongly stressed. However, bear in mind that the indemnity is only worth as much as the equity partners who sign it and may prove worthless if the firm collapses. Without requesting an affidavit of means from each equity partner, it is impossible to guarantee that the indemnity will be worthwhile but you should consider the lifestyle of your prospective partners! A typical clause is as follows:

> The Equity partners hereby jointly and severally covenant to meet all the liabilities of the Firm and hereby indemnify each of the Salaried partners and their respective estates and effects against all claims against him or her in relation to debts, liabilities and obligations of the partnership carried out under the name of A B C & Co.

Notice periods and restrictive covenants

These depend on the firm's size and nature. However, as a general rule, for a salaried partner the notice period should be shorter and the restrictive covenants less onerous than for an equity partner. Most firms consider notice periods of between three and six months as reasonable for a salaried partner. What is a reasonable restrictive covenant depends very much on the nature of the firm's practice, its size and its location.

In general, you may expect the covenants to operate for a period of one year after your employment or appointment terminates, although sometimes it can be as much as three years. The covenants will usually stop you soliciting clients and poaching employees and may prevent you from setting up in competition within a one-mile or more radius of the office. They also restrict reference to the firm's name. If they are too onerous they may be unenforceable but it may be tantamount to asking for litigation to proceed on such an unsafe assumption.

Redundancy

Until the 1990s it was inconceivable that there would be any need for a law firm to make any of its staff redundant and certainly not one or more of its salaried partners. Circumstances and economics change; even equity partners are now not immune to a disappearing work base. For the present, if you are considering or are in the process of negotiating a salaried partnership look carefully at the terms being offered and the effect of your new status on your employment rights.

Unless your firm operates a special structure, it is likely that becoming a salaried partner will not result in you being treated as self-employed for employment purposes. That being the case, your rights remain the same as those of an assistant solicitor faced with redundancy. The exception is where as a salaried partner you enter into a fixed-term contract which contains a contracting-out provision under the Employment Protection (Consolidation) Act 1978 and which is not renewed by the firm at the expiry of the term.

It is not possible here to deal in detail with redundancy rights but the following observations may be of assistance:

(a) Assuming that you have followed the advice in this book and are familiar with the firm, its financial structure and client base, it may be possible to avert the threat of redundancy when the subject is first broached, by offering to transfer yourself (and your talents) to another area of work within the firm. It may be that your partners have already considered this and have come to the conclusion that for some reason this would not be appropriate. Perhaps they view you as too specialised or unwilling to adapt. Whatever the reason, you should have the opportunity to discuss this with them, and suggest alternative areas of work that you feel you would be capable of undertaking.

(b) If the lack of work overall means that alternative employment within the firm is not available, concentrate on negotiating the best possible terms on which to leave. This means not only obvious aspects such as period of notice, and compensation, but also the timing of the announcement to the staff (and the world at large) of the fact that you are leaving and the reason for it. It may be possible to agree with the firm that no announcement be made for a month to give you the opportunity to look for employment elsewhere. Although redundancy is not a reflection on the individual, or their ability (but rather the lack of work), you may wish to be seen to leave for a different reason, particularly if you are negotiating elsewhere. The rules of supply and demand dictate that you will have a stronger hand if you are not perceived as being in need of alternative employment.

(c) Use the opportunity to rethink your career. You may well have been with your firm since the time you undertook your training contract and have viewed partnership as the only goal. If redundancy happens to you, treat it as an opportunity not a setback. With hindsight it may prove to have been the boost you needed to find out what you really wanted to do. The national committee of the YSG continues to operate a helpline to assist young solicitors who are threatened with redundancy. If you need advice you should contact the YSG committee secretary (see 'Useful contacts').

Mergers and takeovers

If a merger or takeover happens it is inevitable that there will be radical changes in the merged firm's structure that will affect you, and possibly your decision to remain there. Although it is likely that your consent to the merger as a salaried partner will not have been required, as a matter of courtesy the equity partners should have consulted you, and on any proposed changes, before they take place. If this did not happen, you need to think very hard about whether these are the partners for you.

With any merger there will be a certain amount of jockeying for position among the equity partners. It is likely that some salaried partners will have become equity partners at the date of the merger. You will need to ascertain what your position is in the scheme of things, and how soon an equity partnership is likely to be offered under the new structure. It is possible that the newly merged firm adopts a different career structure from your old one as a result of which yet another hurdle is put in the way of your becoming an equity partner. Ideally seek a meeting with two or more of the equity partners as soon as the details of the merger have been agreed, with a view to establishing what commitment, if any, they can offer you.

On the plus side a merger can lead to an improved management structure with better career prospects and perhaps an increase in benefits to existing salaried partners. If you are not happy to stay with the new firm, negotiate the terms on which you wish to leave. In particular, if you were asked to enter into a restrictive covenant before becoming a partner, in the circumstances it would not be unreasonable to seek to have this lifted so that you can take up employment elsewhere in the same area.

The route to equity partnership

You need to reach an understanding on when you are likely to be made an equity partner. If your firm is unable or unwilling to give you a timetable for equity partnership, you should question what is the value of your salaried partnership. It is not uncommon, particularly with larger firms, to 'reward' their more profitable (and long-serving employees) with the title of partner, which is in reality salaried and which is never intended to lead any further. The obvious attraction to these firms is that they satisfy the needs of senior assistant solicitors for recognition, while avoiding having to share out the profits.

Obviously your future partners are unlikely to guarantee that within two years you will become an equity partner, but they should make clear to you the time within which you can expect to be offered full partnership, and what would affect that timetable. It is generally useful to speak to more junior equity partners to find out how long it took them to make the transition. Your time as a salaried partner will involve your increased participation in the running of the firm. It will also probably lead to increased social contact with your new partners, which will give them and you a chance to reassess the likelihood of long-term compatibility.

Assuming all goes well, you should expect to receive an offer of equity partnership within the time stated or within a reasonable time of becoming a salaried partner, as a natural progression to your career. If this is not forthcoming or if reality leads you to view the prospect in a different light, then you will have the opportunity to change before you are too committed.

Career progression

This depends largely on your firm. You need to look at its present career structure, existing partners, and the level of commitment being offered to you. It seems to be accepted practice that salaried partnership is the first step to equity partnership. Unless you are being head-hunted from another firm with your own client following, the chances are that you will not be offered an immediate equity partnership.

Before deciding to accept an offer of salaried partnership look at the way in which your firm treats existing salaried partners:

- Are they encouraged to participate in the running of the firm or are they excluded?
- How are they represented to the rest of the staff or to clients?
- What are the financial benefits?
- Are you being asked to give up existing employment rights in return for a fixed-term contract excluding those rights with no guarantee that it will be renewed?

An offer of salaried partnership needs to be considered very carefully bearing in mind the above points. As long as you are happy with the terms on offer, and there is a genuine possibility of progression to equity partnership, you should find the overall advantages outweigh the potential disadvantages.

Do not, however, feel that you have no alternative but to accept on the terms offered. Nor do you have to comply with your firm's timetable, if you feel it appropriate to wait an extra year or so before making an important choice. You have to balance this against the consideration that you do not want to waste an offer, which may not be made twice.

4

Equity partnership

By the time you are considering equity partnership you may already be a salaried partner. Some firms, however, only have one form of status, namely equity partners and other firms even have different strata of equity partnership. An alternative route to equity partnership, which is popular in a depressed economic climate, is that of a sole practitioner, who joins an existing larger firm and comes straight into the firm as an equity partner. However, we can assume if this latter route to equity partnership is taken, the sole practitioner has a good idea of operating and managing a business and so we will not dwell on this particular aspect. It is important to consider your position fully at this stage as equity partnership is thought of as the milestone, when you take on all the responsibilities and liabilities, the good and the bad, jointly and severally with all your partners. Bear in mind that as a partner you will lose the statutory rights you had as an employee concerning any redundancy, unfair dismissal, or maternity leave. Remember you will also have to make provision for your own pension.

Terms of entry

Negotiating your way into partnership will vary greatly from firm to firm and the degree of difficulty may depend on a number of factors. It may well be that you have proved to the existing partners in a short time that you are virtually indispensable and that they have therefore offered you an early partnership and are desperate to get you on board. At the other end of the scale it may be that you have been with the firm for a long time and that you have pressed the firm into offering you a partnership. The degree of negotiating power you have will depend not only on how keen the existing partners are to have you join them but also on the firm's size. The larger the number of existing partners the more likely it is that there will be standard provisions for all partners or a formal career structure. The larger the firm the more frequent will be the coming and going of partners. If this is a frequent occurrence, there is likely to be little or no leeway for individual negotiation of terms. The smaller the firm the more likely you are to be able to negotiate terms specific to you.

The exception to this may well be where a niche practitioner, with his or her own following, is sought by a partnership anxious to gain immediate specialisation in this particular area. Such a practitioner may well be able to dictate his or her own terms of entry into the partnership and even one of the larger firms may allow a different case to be made out in special circumstances.

Whatever your negotiating power, you should ensure that you ask for a copy of the existing partnership agreement if one is in existence. If there is no formal deed, the partners may be prepared to give you a letter outlining the general terms on which the partnership operates for you to respond to by way of acceptance. This latter aspect is dealt with in more detail in Chapter 8.

Know your firm

As mentioned in earlier chapters, to a certain extent how well you know your firm will depend on how large the firm is and whether there are several offices. You will need to think of the individuals with whom you are hoping to enter partnership and whether you feel you can work with them as your partners. The human element is all-important in a partnership. If there is a particular partner with whose views you do not agree, you may still be happy to enter the partnership on the basis that he or she has very little contact with you and that you get on with the majority of the partners.

If, however, you do not get on with somebody with whom you will have to work closely, then this may affect your decision whether to enter the partnership. There may be some partners who work long hours at the office and bring in substantial fees. There may be other partners who do not appear to put in the same hours of work but may have an ability to attract substantial work to the firm from their social activities and contacts. No two partners are likely to put the same effort, in the same way, into the partnership but you should establish whether their abilities complement each other and provide a sound basis of talent on which to build. This may be easier to find in good times. The strength of a good partnership is that they all stay together and help each other through the bad times.

You will need to ask yourself whether you are happy with the standard of work of the other partners and whether you trust them all. As mentioned previously you need to check the firm's professional indemnity cover (see Chapter 1 and Chapter 15). If the list of claims has a common source, perhaps in respect of one particular partner, then it should ring alarm bells. Check whether the insurance cover has been increased by any 'top-up', bearing in mind the type of work the partnership undertakes.

Look also at the firm's administrative arrangements and ensure you are either happy with the structure or that you are confident your views will be fully considered by your fellow partners should you enter into partnership. In particular, ask the partners if they have a business development plan, which should indicate where the partners see the firm heading within the next five years, the type of clientele and casework they are aiming to promote, and their strategy in terms of the partnership's development. Consider the firm's attitude to computer technology and whether it is up to date. Question whether there is a maintenance agreement in force for the computer hardware and ascertain whether there are any foreseeable requirements for heavy investment, perhaps in a new system or replacement of a substantial amount of machinery in the short term.

Consider the firm's administrative efficiency in recovering bad debts and check office procedures to ensure partners receive a regular update on outstanding accounts. Remember, bad debts can severely affect cash flow, which in turn will affect your drawings and may mean that the capital of the business in which you are being invited to invest quite simply is not there.

Ask for details of the freehold and leasehold premises from which the partnership operates. If some of the partners own the freehold outside the partnership and lease it to the partnership, you will need to consider what might happen if the freehold owners retire from the partnership and decide to sell the property for redevelopment. Look at any leasehold interests and check when the next rent review is due. Enquire as to whether the partnership owns any properties which are vacant, but upon which they are still paying rent while trying to sell. In times of economic recession it is unlikely that new tenants will be found and this may prove an unexpected liability.

Finally, look at the partnership structure. Are all the existing partners of similar ages or is there a good range within the practice? An ideal practice should have a good separation of ages with younger people continuously coming through the ranks. Remember if there is a bunching of ages ahead of you it may mean there is no opportunity for you to increase your profit ratio for some time. Additionally, when partners retire within a short period of each other, it may put excessive strain on the firm's capital. Consider whether there is a senior partner with heavy investment in the firm, who is likely to want to retire and withdraw that investment. What provisions have the other partners made for this?

Limited liability partnerships

Definition

The Limited Liability Partnerships Act 2000 introduced a new form of legal entity. The limited liability partnership is brought into being when two or more people (members) incorporate themselves as a limited liability partnership. The key elements of a limited liability partnership are that it is a body corporate and has unlimited capacity but that the members' liability is limited to what has been agreed beforehand. It therefore protects an individual member from liability for acts carried out in the course of the business. It differs from a company in that it can have a decision-making and profit-sharing structure drawn up for its purpose, which will be a private agreement between members. The limited liability partnership will, however, be subject to various provisions of the Companies Act 1985 but not those about meetings and resolutions, management and share capital.

The name of a limited liability partnership must end with those same words or the abbreviation 'LLP' (or llp). The name must be different from any existing name on the index of names kept by the Registrar of Companies.

Default agreement

There is no requirement to have a formal agreement but the default provisions are:

(a) all members entitled to equal shares of capital and profits;
(b) an indemnity to members in respect of partnership expenses;
(c) all members to take part in management, no entitlement to pay in respect of management duties;
(d) all existing members have to agree on admission of new members or the assignment of another member's interest;
(e) members cannot be expelled without all the members' express agreement;

(f) majority decisions are required, other than changes to the nature of business where all members' agreement is required;

(g) all members to have access to the books and records; and

(h) members cannot compete against the partnership without consent.

Advantages and disadvantages

The main advantage is the protection from liability but this is gained at a price. The limited liability partnership has a duty to file annual accounts, an auditor's report and an annual return with the Registrar of Companies. The return must be filed 12 months after incorporation and not more than 12 months after the previous return. The limited liability partnership will also need to file notices of change of membership. If the limited liability partnership defaults in any of these obligations, then the Registrar of Companies may serve a notice requiring it to deliver the document or give the notice. If the partnership does not take this step within 14 days after service of the notice, then the Registrar may apply to court for an order to remedy the default.

The Registrar also publishes in the *London Gazette* notices of issue or receipt of the certificate of incorporation, any document changing incorporation, any notification of membership changes, any accounts or reports delivered, any change of registered office, any copy of a winding-up order and any return by a liquidator of the final meeting of the limited liability partnership. It is these features which leads many partners, used to keeping business matters confidential, to be reluctant to pursue this form of organisation.

Another disadvantage from many partners' perspective is the limited liability partnership is subject to the Companies Act 1985 regime, i.e. subject to investigation by the Department for Trade and Industry. Members will also be subject to the Company Directors Disqualification Act 1986 and, if the partnership goes into liquidation, they will also be subject to the 'wrongful trading' and similar provisions of the Insolvency Act 1986.

For tax purposes, the limited liability partnership is treated as a partnership and the members as partners. However, it is not the position that in default of express terms, partnership law applies. All business letters and documents should show the full name, place of registration and registered number and the registered office address. Where there are fewer than 20 members, the names of all the members must be shown on stationery. If a limited liability partnership has more than 20 members, it can choose not to give all the names but must provide an address at which the list of members' names can be viewed.

Terms of agreement

Many of the terms will be similar to those in an ordinary partnership (see Chapter 8) but they should also include terms on incorporation and the duties to file returns and accounts with Companies House. They should also include a term about changing the name or registered office. There may be more complex terms relating to the management of the partnership meetings.

It should be noted that not many firms have taken up the opportunity to limit their liability by adopting this form of partnership despite the obvious advantages of limiting the threat to partners' own assets.

Further information

More information is available from Professional Ethics, the Law Society. They produce an information pack called *Incorporated Practice: LLPs* (see 'Useful contacts').

6

Incorporated practices

Introduction

Section 9 of the Administration of Justice Act 1985 permits solicitors to practise through a body corporate. The body corporate must first be formally recognised by the Law Society as a 'recognised body' under rule 21(1) of the Solicitors' Incorporated Practice Rules 2001. There are two types of body corporate in England and Wales – a company (limited or unlimited) and a limited liability partnership (LLP). Both are eligible to become recognised bodies.

If your firm is considering incorporation you will wish to give detailed consideration to the taxation aspects with your and the firm's advisers, and to a variety of other matters affecting any business on incorporation, for example the effects on any lease of office premises and the firm's borrowing.

Rules

The Solicitors' Incorporated Practice Rules 2001 cover technical matters including the location of a recognised body's registered office, the ownership of shares and the composition of the board of directors of a company, the membership of an LLP, the application of the rules and principles of conduct, and how applications for recognition should be made. A company must be incorporated in England and Wales, or incorporated in another European state and registered at Companies House as an overseas company. An LLP must be incorporated by registration at Companies House.

Only solicitors, registered European lawyers, registered foreign lawyers and certain other European lawyers may participate in a recognised body as directors, members or shareowners.

Fees and Compensation Fund contributions

As at November 2002 the fee for recognition as a recognised body is £500. The recognised body also has to pay a contribution to the Compensation Fund of £400. Both these fees are payable every three years.

In addition all solicitors who are directors, members, shareowners or employees must pay practising certificate fees and Compensation Fund contributions. Those solicitors who are directors, members or shareowners pay Compensation Fund contributions on the same basis as if they were principals in the practice.

Professional indemnity

The Solicitors' Indemnity Insurance Rules 2002 require recognised bodies to have qualifying insurance for a minimum of £1 million for each and every claim, in the same way as other practices.

Rule 18 of the Solicitors' Incorporated Practice Rules 2001 requires a recognised body which is a limited company or LLP to take out top-up cover of £500,000 for each and every claim or £2 million per year on an aggregate basis.

Further information

Two information packs on incorporated practices – one on companies, and one on LLPs – are available from Professional Ethics at the Law Society (see 'Useful contacts').

Application forms for recognition of a body corporate as a recognised body may be obtained from the Registration Department, also at the Law Society (see 'Useful contacts').

Multi-disciplinary partnerships

As yet the solicitors' profession has set its face against the concept of multi-disciplinary partnerships (MDPs). This is not a position supported by the national committee of the YSG. It seems that despite the removal of the statutory prohibition on MDPs effected by the Courts and Legal Services Act 1990, little progress has been made although the matter is under review.

Our belief is that any move towards MDPs is likely to be accountancy driven. Already the major international accountancy firms employ more lawyers in house in England than there are practising at the bar. This trend is likely to continue and we expect that the major accountancy firms will become, if they have not already become, de facto MDPs whether they remain firms of accountants or not.

Multi-disciplinary partnerships are based on the premise that the client wishes to have 'one stop shopping' (a total business advisory service under one roof) and undoubtedly there is a niche in the market for the provision of legal and other business advisory services in this manner. The accountants do not, for obvious reasons, seem interested in MDPs which would deliver private client services and would not wish to be involved in any legal aid or pro bono work. If you are faced with the prospect of your firm linking up with, for example, a firm of accountants to form an MDP, you should bear such factors in mind, particularly if your field of work includes legal aid work or other less profitable areas of private client work.

In general solicitors in private practice seem to have found little to attract them to the idea of becoming part of an MDP. In our view, however, it is inevitable that these will come about, although their effect in relation to the profession may have been over-dramatised to the same extent as the cataclysmic effect promised by those opposing the abolition of the residential conveyancing monopoly. We are happy to see MDPs come into existence and are confident that the delivery of legal services will not be materially affected provided there are suitable safeguards for the public, particularly in such problem areas as conflicts of interest.

We believe that the practice rules and regulations of the profession can be altered in a similar way as has been done for multinational partnerships in order to provide a framework for the existence of MDPs.

Rather than try to create a single common code for members of different professions who might practise in partnership together, it is our view that each partner should remain individually subject to the rules of his or her own professional body and assume personal responsibility for the activities of the practice within his or her own professional field.

This does, however, give rise to a potential problem as to the nature of the various professional groups which may band together to form an MDP and this factor may be the most difficult to overcome.

Certainly, each professional body must have adequate powers of a disciplinary nature to ensure that any defaulting professionals could be debarred from further practice and that a particular MDP could be deprived of the right to include a particular category of professional. This would of course require liaison between the various professional bodies, in particular to ensure a consistency of approach to disciplinary matters.

Conclusion

The YSG said as long ago as 1987 that it saw no conflict between the concept of MDPs and a solicitor's absolute obligation to act in the client's interest and with the utmost integrity: 'where the solicitor's professional duty conflicted with that of his or her partners, irrespective of who they are or the majority involved; the duty to the client (and to the court) would always prevail'.

8

The partnership agreement

What to look for in the partnership agreement

Whether or not the partnership has a partnership agreement (and it certainly should do) read through this chapter very carefully. The formal agreement should cover the principal aspects of the operation of the partnership and your relationship to the other partners. Most firms vary their partnership agreement from time to time and with large, ever evolving practices the partnership agreement could change frequently, with the consent of the partners. Bear in mind that under the Partnership Act 1890, s.19:

> The mutual rights and duties of partners, whether ascertained by agreement or defined by this Act, may be varied by the consent of all the partners, and such consent may be either express or inferred from a course of dealing.

So even a partnership deed can be varied by custom and practice.

When reading a partnership agreement, the clauses fall naturally into various groups, although they are rarely organised in a logical way. The following sections describe some typical groups of clauses that you should find in an agreement.

General and inter-partner clauses

Duration

It is important that the duration of the partnership is defined, as otherwise the partnership will be a 'partnership at will', which can be dissolved at any time by one partner giving notice to the others. It is usual to provide that the partnership continues during the joint lives of any two or more partners and that the death, retirement, expulsion or any other reason whereby a partner ceases to remain as a partner shall not determine a partnership as regards the other parties. The agreement will also contain provisions concerning periods of notice to retire.

General duties and restrictions

All agreements have clauses that establish the duty of good faith between partners which is the essence of partnership. These include a statement of good faith, a requirement to work full time for the firm, and not to compete with it. Restrictions are limits on the authority of a partner to commit the firm without authority from other partners. Typically there are restrictions on hiring and firing staff, entering into major financial commitments and exposing the firm to financial risk arising from a partner's personal circumstances.

Holidays

It is usual for any partnership agreement to provide for the number of weeks' holiday each partner should have each year; one would expect these to be more than for employed staff. However, in smaller firms this may not apply.

Maternity and sabbaticals

Both male and female prospective partners should consider what effect any provision for maternity leave (or lack of it) will have on the future running of the firm and its ability to attract female partners and qualified staff.

The Association of Women Solicitors has put forward a suggested form of wording for a maternity clause provision in a partnership agreement which your firm may well be willing to adopt if it does not already have its own. A copy may be obtained by contacting the Association's Committee Secretary at the Law Society (see 'Useful contacts').

The question of sabbaticals is addressed in Chapter 2.

Arbitration

Provision should be made in the partnership agreement for any dispute affecting partnership matters to be referred to arbitration. The common form of arbitration clause can be suitably adapted and used in this connection.

Financial arrangements

Capital

All firms require partners to contribute capital to the firm. These are funds that the firm needs to help maintain its cash flow and finance its assets. Capital is a fixed investment in the firm, normally payable on becoming a partner, and only repayable on leaving the firm. Some firms require partners to borrow the funds for their capital, and some larger firms allow partners to contribute their capital by restricting drawings until the relevant amount has been subscribed. Normally, partners contribute capital in proportion to their profit shares – if you are entitled to 10 per cent of the profits, you would expect to contribute 10 per cent of capital. Goodwill payments are unusual in modern agreements (see 'Repayment of capital and indemnity' later in this chapter). When you become a partner in a firm, you accept liability for all of the historical obligations of the firm jointly and severally with the ongoing partners. Insist on seeing the accounts and make certain that you carry out appropriate due diligence to ensure that you are not taking on unexpected financial obligations (you should take advice on this).

Profit shares

The agreement will set out how the net profit of the firm is divided. There are many different ways of dividing profits. Some may divide profits equally, though this is by no means the common method. The traditional method in larger firms is lockstep. This is a points ladder which partners climb automatically each year so that after, say ten years, they reach parity with the senior partners. Some smaller firms are more likely to have fixed partnership shares and you are unlikely to be able to increase your partnership share without the departure of an existing partner. Other firms have a system of rewards dependent on each partner's performance, responsibilities, length of service within the partnership or any other factor which a particular partnership wishes to take into account.

Many have permutations of some or all of the above. Whichever is used, you should satisfy yourself that:

- you should be in a better position than you were as an assistant solicitor or salaried partner (bearing in mind the need to finance capital); and
- it is clear how you are to progress and hence increase your share of the profits.

Drawings

A partner does not receive a salary, and technically is not entitled to any payment until after each year's accounts are signed, when the profits can be distributed. However, in every firm there are arrangements for drawings (regular payments on account of expected profits). When the firm's annual accounts are signed the balance of a year's profits are distributed, less the drawings already received. If you have overdrawn, you will be expected to repay the overdrawing. In many firms the balance of profits is not all distributed. Profits are not cash in the bank (they are based on bills delivered – not cash received) and the firm can only distribute what it can afford. Frequently there are reserves for anticipated expenditure before distribution, especially if the firm is expanding. Someone (you!) has to pay the salaries of new staff until they start paying their way.

Benefits

Any specific benefits provided to a partner may well appear in the partnership agreement. Common benefits may be private health insurance and sometimes the provision of a car with all expenses paid by the partnership. In city centre practice the provision of a car is no longer common, as the cost cannot be justified for tax purposes. Bear in mind that there are no real benefits for partners: each so-called benefit paid out reduces the profit, so what you receive as a benefit you may well lose as a profit share.

Management and administration

The agreement will provide for voting majorities on different issues, varying between unanimity and straight majorities. Serious issues like admission of new partners, expulsions, variation of the agreement and dissolution require large majorities. Other issues, for example bank mandates, need only a simple majority.

It is more common in larger practices to see provision in the partnership agreement for a structured system of management and administration. This may involve the appointment of senior and managing partners and management committees responsible for the running of the firm and collating the views of all other partners. It may provide for various committees to be set up to deal with different aspects of the partnership such as marketing and strategy planning. However, with smaller practices it is likely that the various tasks involved with the management and administration are allocated to respective partners on an informal basis without mention in the partnership agreement. Many agreements for smaller firms contain provisions appointing senior and managing partners without specifying their authority.

Leaving the firm

Retirement and compulsory retirement

The agreement will provide for the period of notice to be given before a partner can leave the firm (rarely less than six months) and for an automatic retirement age. Many agreements provide for 'compulsory retirement' (a power for a majority of the partners to force another partner to leave), usually without any reason being specified. Remember that partners are not employees, so no claim for unfair dismissal can be brought. Agreements also contain provisions for compulsory retirement of partners who are incapacitated for an extended period, say six months. If there is no formal partnership agreement, then the partnership will be a partnership at will and, in the absence of agreement, a partner can leave only by dissolving the partnership (as set out below).

Expulsion

As the Partnership Act 1890 provides that no majority of partners can expel any partner unless a power to do so has been conferred by express agreement between the partners, every agreement should contain a specific power to expel a partner. Normal grounds for expulsion are, for example, bankruptcy, criminal conduct, wilful neglect of his or her duties, substantial breach of the agreement, being struck off and other matters similar to those for which an employee would be subject to summary dismissal.

Restrictive covenants

In any partnership agreement, you would expect to see restrictive covenants preventing any partner who is leaving the partnership from:

- acting for, or soliciting any, client of the partnership;
- enticing or endeavouring to entice an employee from the firm; and
- practising as a solicitor within a specified radius from any office of the partnership.

In order to be enforceable, restrictive covenants must be reasonable, but the courts are generally supportive of covenants between partners, as they are regarded as being agreements between equals (especially as everyone who seeks to enforce a covenant is also subject to it). Obviously the covenants should be for a reasonable duration, say one to two years and, in the case of distance restrictions, for a reasonable distance. With major city centre practice, distance restrictions are probably unenforceable, as they are designed to protect local and passing trade practice. However, assume that any restrictions, however draconian, will be enforceable. Entirely different, and more stringent, tests of reasonableness apply to salaried partners who are employees.

Repayment of capital and indemnity

The agreement will set out the terms on which a retiring partner is to be repaid his or her capital by the firm, as well as the balance of profits for the year in which he or she leaves. Periods of up to three years are quite common to allow the partnership to carry on functioning without the withdrawal causing cash flow problems, and to ensure compliance with restrictive covenants. Interest is normally paid on outstanding capital. Payments for goodwill are unusual in modern solicitors practices as are annuities to retiring partners, and you should be wary of entering into agreements which contain such provisions, as these can give rise to substantial financial commitments by you. The agreement will also contain an indemnity to the outgoing partner for all liabilities of the firm whether or not known at the retirement date. As soon as a partner retires, his or her capital and profit share, and the indemnity become personal liabilities of the other partners which survive even a dissolution of the practice.

Dissolution

You would expect to find provision in a partnership agreement for the existing partners to resolve to dissolve the partnership on either a majority or unanimous vote. Such a provision should then give details of how it is proposed to divide the net surplus assets of the firm once dissolved (usually in profit-sharing ratios).

Salaried partner indemnity

In the case of a new entrant to salaried partnership an indemnity should be taken from the full equity partners in respect of liabilities assumed by the salaried partner to the outside world by appearing on the notepaper as a partner. Within the partnership such liabilities should only be borne by those entitled to a share of the profits. Although such an indemnity is some comfort to a salaried partner, it must not be forgotten that if the equity partners have insufficient assets to cover the liabilities, the indemnity will not protect the salaried partner from liability to any third party. A specimen clause and further advice appear in Chapter 3.

Informal partnership agreements

Even if there is no formal detailed partnership agreement, a partnership still exists at law. Its terms could be ascertained from a combination of letters, memos, minutes, conduct and the terms implied into the partnership by the Partnership Act 1890. Take the greatest care before becoming partner in such a firm, as even a two-person firm needs to have some agreement as to dissolution arrangements if the partners fall out.

9

Independent advice

It is recommended that you take professional advice about the firm's accounts and also about the partnership agreement and general terms of the offer. It could be that you have a friend, who is either a solicitor or an accountant, perhaps in another town, removed from the immediate geographical area of your practice, whose opinion you value and who is already a partner having gone through a similar experience. He or she can probably advise you informally and impartially and reassure you over any doubts you may have.

If you have no such acquaintance or friend, then you should consider instructing an accountant and/or solicitor professionally. You may prefer to choose someone outside your immediate geographical area of practice. It is an important step in your career, especially in financial terms, and as such justifies incurring fees for professional advice. All partnerships operate slightly differently so do not be deterred if the experiences of persons you confide in are not the same as yours.

The national committee of the YSG offers an advice scheme for those entering into partnership. For more details of this scheme you should contact the Policy Manager for the YSG at the Law Society (see 'Useful contacts').

Volunteers on the Solicitors Assistance Scheme (SAS) can also provide help on partnership and finance issues. A list of their members can be obtained from the Law Society (see 'Useful contacts').

Accounts

What to look for in partnership accounts

You will want to see the accounts for at least three years. However if you join the firm without seeing any accounts you will be neither the first nor the last to do so. You may feel that you are honoured to receive an invitation to join the firm as a partner and that you have no bargaining position. However, the firm wants you and it needs new partners to ensure its continued survival and to help pay for partners as they pass their peak in earning capacity and, perhaps, for their future pensions. Changes in the property market, in commerce and legal aid may mean that firms who have prospered in the past may not be well equipped to prosper in the future.

If you are offered an equity partnership, you may be invited to pay a substantial sum to purchase an asset and your future career. It is not unreasonable to ask that you be allowed to see what you are buying. You may have gained much knowledge about the firm as an employee, but to become an equity partner without seeing the accounts may be likened to buying a used car for its appearance without taking a test drive – you know what it looks like but you do not know how well it works. A partnership can only function properly with openness. If your future partners will not let you see the accounts you must ask yourself whether they are hiding anything from you and whether this indicates an environment in which you might not wish to work in the future. Some of the points you should look for are set out below.

Assets

You should look at the balance sheet to see what assets are included. The firm may practise from valuable freehold premises for example, but if the premises are owned by a senior partner who allows the firm to use them with or without paying rent, there is a substantial asset in which you will not be acquiring an interest (except perhaps as a protected business tenant) when you contribute to the capital of the firm. Furthermore, problems may arise when the partner who owns the property retires. Even if the retiring partner is prepared to allow the firm to stay there, perhaps at less than a full commercial rent, there may be problems when he or she dies, perhaps unexpectedly before retirement. If freehold property is owned by the firm and appears in the books at cost, consideration may be given to revaluation but there may be capital gains tax consequences, which are explained in more detail in Chapter 11. If leasehold property appears in the accounts is there any premium value? Are there onerous covenants in the lease? In either case you may wish to consider the structural condition of the property and, if leasehold, the repairing obligations.

Goodwill

It is unlikely these days that you will find goodwill in the accounts of any professional partnership. However, if it is to be written off, the existing partners may require compensation and there may be capital gains tax implications upon which you need to seek specialist taxation advice. If goodwill is being written off when you join the firm, the existing partners might be compensated by provision in the partnership agreement for pensions to be paid to them in the future.

Annuities

You should enquire what current or future commitments the firm has to pay annuities or other capital sums to retired partners. This may have profound implications for the future profitability and indebtedness of the firm. This may be particularly important if there are several partners approaching retirement.

Work in progress

Work in progress will only appear in the accounts of the firm drawn up on the earnings basis, which is explained briefly in Chapter 11. If work in progress is included in the accounts you will want to be sure that it is valued on a basis which is consistent year by year and that it is not being used as a device to inflate the apparent profitability of the firm.

Bad debts

You will want to be satisfied as to what provision has been made for bad or doubtful debts in the debtors figure and that provisions have been consistent year by year. You should not be paying for a share of debts owed to the firm which have no realistic prospect of being recovered. Similarly, you must ensure that all known or contingent liabilities have been brought into account.

If the accounts are prepared on a cash basis, as explained below, debtors in respect of fees rendered but unpaid would not appear in the balance sheet nor would unpaid debts of the firm. You must ensure that the firm has a satisfactory procedure for recovering outstanding debts. It has to be said, however, that a high proportion of actions for unpaid fees result in counter-claims being made for alleged professional negligence and it is highly desirable that the firm has a policy of another partner reviewing a file before an action is commenced to recover fees.

Fixtures and fittings

Fixtures and fittings may in fact be worth little or nothing, even though depreciation has been allowed for them in the accounts. Expensive fitted furniture may only be of any value in your firm's office and of little practical value elsewhere.

Cars

You must find out whether partners' cars are treated as assets of the firm and, if so, what provision will be made for you. Cars may be at the discretion of the partner or the subject of complex provisions in the partnership agreement.

Net current assets

The accounts will probably show net current assets but if not, you can calculate the amount. It is useful to do so because the figure represents the excess of current assets (those which can be fairly quickly turned into cash) over current liabilities (those obligations that must be paid for in the foreseeable future). A narrow margin of current assets over current liabilities may indicate actual or potential cash flow problems and may mean that the firm needs further capital.

Accounts are historical

Remember that accounts provide only a historical perspective and matters may have changed significantly since the period covered. This is particularly important if the historic results may have been improved significantly by non-recurring fee income.

Profit and loss

You should also review the profit and loss accounts. These record the firm's income and expenses, the difference being profit before taxation available for partners.

Income may be recognised on one of three bases: cash, earnings (or work done/accruals basis) or bills delivered. These are described in Chapter 11. Only if the firm uses the earnings basis will work in progress appear in the balance sheet. The basis of recognising income in accounts will normally follow the earnings basis, as this is the style of reporting employed for tax purposes.

You should remember that if you were already an employee of the firm (whether as an assistant or as a salaried partner) the figure for wages in the profit and loss accounts would include your salary and any bonus that you receive. This will be one item of expense which will not be incurred when you become an equity partner and will represent an additional cash sum available for distribution.

Management accounts

A well run firm will also have management accounts prepared periodically, probably monthly, to enable partners to see how the firm is progressing throughout the year.

You will expect these accounts to include a budget of the fees that the partners expect to generate, the expenses they expect to incur during the year, a reporting system, which compares what actually happens with that which was planned, and sufficient information to enable partners to take any necessary remedial action during the course of the year. It is no use finding out the situation after the year-end when the annual accounts have been prepared. Most computerised account systems will be able to provide the required information.

If you are concerned about the future cash flow or liquidity of the firm or its profitability, you should inspect these projections to see whether problems may arise, and whether projected profitability is in line with your expectations. You should consider whether the basis of preparation of the projections and any assumptions made are reasonable in the light of your own knowledge and experience of the partnership and its client base.

Other sources of income

You will see from the partnership agreement whether partners are required to bring into account, and from the accounts whether they in fact do so, income from other sources such as part-time judicial appointments, directors' fees, commissioners' fees and royalties from publications.

Similarly, is there any source of income (or indeed expenditure) of which you were not aware, and if so, what is its nature?

Service companies

Ask if there is a service company owned by some or all of the partners, which provides services to the partnership for a fee. For example, a service company may provide or operate the premises, or provide staff, secretarial or computer facilities. You will need to enquire into the details of such an arrangement. If you are to become a director you must ensure the company has complied with its obligation, particularly under the Companies Act, in view of the increasing burdens placed on directors by the law.

The way partnership accounting works

The balance sheet and the profit and loss account will be in the same form as they would be for any other business. However, they will also have to show the finances as they affect individual partners. You will, therefore, find that they include partners' capital accounts, current accounts and taxation accounts.

The level of capital required will normally be specified in the partnership agreement. There may be provision for you to pay your initial capital in instalments. There may be a requirement to pay further capital in the future, possibly annually. The agreement may provide for withdrawal of capital but this is probably uncommon before leaving the firm.

The capital accounts will show the balance at the beginning of the financial year, any additional capital introduced during the year and, usually in the case of retiring partners, any capital withdrawn. They will then show the balance at the year-end. Capital introduced may have been brought in from outside the firm by a partner or may have been transferred internally from their current account; this may appear in the capital and current accounts.

The current accounts will show for each partner the balance at the beginning of the year and their share of profit. On the debit side there will be drawings paid during the year, any money withheld for taxation provision and any sums transferred to partners' capital accounts as mentioned above. Finally, they show the balance at the year-end, hopefully as a credit owed by the firm to the partners.

Overdrawn loan accounts are normally to be discouraged, particularly as they risk a disallowance of part of the tax relief otherwise available for interest on partnership borrowings.

Taxation accounts cover the income tax liability. Income tax is assessed individually on the partners of the firm. There is no requirement to reserve for income tax in the partnership accounts (unless provided for in the partnership agreement) but it is good practice, particularly in larger practices. Reserves have to be kept to pay the tax when it falls due, which may be anything up to 21 months after the end of the accounting year in which the fees are earned. The firm therefore needs to reserve funds to pay tax bills and this topic is discussed in Chapter 11. The taxation accounts in the accounts of the partnership will show for each partner the balance held to his or her credit (hopefully not a debit) at the beginning of the year. As a debit they will show any sums paid out to the Revenue on each partner's behalf during the year and as a credit they will show any further sums which have been retained from each partner's share of profit by way of provision for future tax liabilities.

Finally the accounts will show the balance held to the credit of each partner at the year-end.

You should ensure that the accountant's certificate has been completed, and that no concerns were expressed. Although an audit on the firm's client account is mandatory it is unusual for a firm to have an audit on the firm's office account. Any practice which incorporates with limited liability, however, will need to have an audit to comply with the Companies Act.

Complying with the Solicitors' Accounts Rules 1998

Remember that as a partner you would be individually responsible for the compliance of the whole firm with the Solicitors' Accounts Rules and Deposit Interest Rules. The issue of your practising certificate is dependent on the proper recording and control of clients' monies within the requirements of the Rules. While, in practice, it may have to be left on a day-to-day basis to the firm's cash department, the responsibility for compliance remains with you.

It is essential to ensure that the client account is reconciled with the bank statements monthly (the Rules require this to be done at least once every 14 weeks for controlled trust money held in passbook-operated separate designated client accounts, and at least once every five weeks in all other cases). You should enquire what controls are imposed on drawing cheques whether on client or office account. For your own preservation there should be limits on the amount for which one partner can sign and there should be no accounts under the control of one partner alone. There should be limits on the disbursements which can be incurred on behalf of clients without being reimbursed promptly or paid out of money held on account – you should be your client's solicitor not a banker.

You must ensure that monies required to be paid into the firm's client account are not paid into the office account, particularly noting the position of unbilled disbursements. Under the Solicitors' Accounts Rules 1998, where a bill includes disbursements which have not yet been paid upon payment of the bill, that part of the money which relates to the unpaid disbursements must be paid into the client account and not the office account unless, and until, the disbursements are paid. Disbursements subject to VAT will have to be paid out of the office account if the firm is to recover the VAT on them.

For publicly funded firms any claims on account of disbursements can be credited to the office account. If the disbursement remains unpaid after 14 days, then the amount claimed must be transferred to the client account. If the firm is not making certain that this occurs then it is an indication of poor financial management systems.

You should also remember that under the Solicitors' Accounts Rules, clients' receipts must be paid into the firm's client account on the day of receipt or the following day.

Remember above all else, that the issue of your practising certificate depends on compliance with the Rules.

Taxation

Partnership taxation is a complex subject and this chapter is therefore for guidance only and represents a brief overview. You should take advice from your taxation adviser if in doubt. Tax law and practice changes rapidly. The law is stated as at 2 September 2002 and you should check in particular whether there have been any changes since then.

How firms are taxed

Since the introduction of self assessment there are no longer partnership assessments. Instead partners will be assessed on their share of the partnership profits. Partnerships are still required to file a partnership tax return that is subject to the same enquiry procedures as an individual.

Partners' profits are charged to income tax for each tax year, which runs from 6 April in one year to 5 April in the following year. The assessment for the year is based upon a partner's share of profits earned in the accounting year ending in the year under assessment so, for example, if an established firm prepares its accounts to 31 December each year the assessment for the tax year 2002–03 (commencing 6 April 2002) would be based upon the partner's share of profits for the year to 31 December 2002. This is known as the 'current year' basis.

A complete change in the ownership of a continuing business will trigger a deemed cessation under Income and Corporation Taxes Act 1988, s.113(1). But, where there is only a partial change in the ownership of a continuing business a 'deemed continuation' rule will automatically apply.

Taxation in the year of joining the partnership

The above is applicable for existing partners but not for a new partner in the year of joining an established firm. The entrant will be subject to taxation on the 'actual basis' in the tax year of joining; this is the period from the date of joining in a tax year until the end of that fiscal year.

Taking the above example of an existing firm with a 31 December year-end and allowing for a partner joining 1 January 2002. Their assessments for the 2001–02 tax year (6 April 2001 to 5 April 2002) would be as follows:

> The new partner's share of profits for the accounting year 31 December 2002 pro-rata for the period 1 January 2002 to 5 April 2002. In the second year of assessment 2002–03 tax year (6 April 2002 to 5 April 2003) the 'new' entrant's profits are subject to the normal 'current year' basis rules.

Their assessments for the 2002–03 tax year (6 April 2002 to 5 April 2003) would be as follows:

> The new partner's share of profits for the entire accounting year to 31 December 2002.

The more astute reader will have noticed that the new entrant's share of profit for the period 1 January 2002 to 5 April 2002 is being taxed twice. This breaches one of the fundamental tenets of taxation, that profits of a business should only be taxed once. This fact was recognised when the self assessment regime was designed; in an attempt to give a measure of relief the concept of 'overlap' profits has been introduced.

Overlap profit is the partner's share of profit for the period 1 January 2002 to 5 April 2002, which has been taxed initially in the 2001–02 tax year on the 'actual' basis and subsequently in the 2002–03 tax year on the 'current year' basis. The overlap profit once ascertained, may be recorded on the partner's tax return and carried forward until such time as the partner leaves the firm. In the tax year of departure the 'overlap' profit brought forward may be deducted from the leaver's share of profit assessable, even to the extent where a loss arises.

There are a number of exceptions to the above, two of which are:

1. Where the accounting period in the second year of assessment ends less than 12 months after a new partner joins the firm. In which case the first year's assessment will remain on the 'actual' basis, while the second year of assessment will change from the 'current year' basis to a basis that will encompass the first 12 months of assessable profit accrued by the new entrant.
2. Where the accounting date in the second year falls more than 12 months from the date of joining. In which case the basis of assessment in the second year is the 12 months to the accounting period end.

It should also be noted that there would be an impact on the calculation of 'overlap' profits but to avoid overcomplication we do not propose to go into greater depth in what is meant only to be an outline.

For income tax purposes, when a partner leaves or joins, the partnership is treated as continuing and therefore there is no change in the basis of assessment. All existing partners' profits will be assessed on the current year basis while the new member's profits will be assessed on an 'actual' basis from the date of joining until the end of the tax year in being at that time, then on the 'current year' basis (as previously described).

The above is an oversimplification for the purpose of this book. Firms should seek timely advice from a taxation adviser ahead of any changes either in the number of partners or the share of profits between partners and when considering a change in their accounting date.

Basis of accounting

As mentioned in Chapter 10, partnership accounts can be compiled in one of three ways:

- cash basis – excludes work in progress and debtors;
- bills delivered basis – excludes work in progress, includes debtors;
- earnings basis (accrual basis) – includes work in progress and debtors.

For accounting periods of established professional practices up to and including the period ending in the tax year 1999–2000, the Inland Revenue accepted that work in progress did not need to be included. However, for an accounting period commencing in the 1999–2000 tax year, work in progress has to be included. It is therefore most likely that partnership accounts are prepared using the earnings basis.

Profits and losses will be computed at partnership level (ICTA 1988, s.111(2)) using income tax rules applicable to individuals. Once calculated, the assessable profits are then allocated, in accordance with the partnership profit share ratio to the respective individual partners for declaration on their individual tax returns.

When income tax is payable

Assuming that prior to taking up an option to become a partner in a firm you were previously self-employed and not required to file tax returns you will be required to pay income tax twice yearly, on 31 January and 31 July. This can be best illustrated using the circumstances set out above in 'Taxation in the year of joining the partnership' (see p.61).

A tax return will be issued on 6 April 2002 by the Inland Revenue on which you will be required to report all taxable income, either earned or derived from savings and investments, as well as chargeable capital gains/losses arising during the 2001–02 tax year. Personal tax returns must be returned to the Inspector of Taxes by the 30 September following the tax year-end, if you wish him to calculate your liability, or the following 31 January if you or your agent intend to carry out the calculation. It should be noted that the Inland Revenue has the potential to levy penalties for late returns and since the advent of the self assessment regime these will be imposed automatically, with little chance of a successful appeal.

Any balance of income tax outstanding for the 2001–02 tax year arising on submission of the 2002 tax return will be due payable on or by 31 January 2003. It should be noted that one of the fundamental changes self assessment introduced in 1996–97 was a shift in responsibilities. The Inland Revenue is no longer responsible for the issue of assessments, this burden has been passed to the taxpayer. As a result, a taxpayer can no longer wait to receive a tax demand from the Inland Revenue; they must now make sure that any liability arising is paid on, or by, the due date(s) even if the return has not been processed. If the income tax payable for the expired tax year is greater than £500 the payment is not only to make settlement by the due date but also to make a payment on account at the same time towards the following tax year (current tax year). This payment on account is 50 per cent of the preceding year's balance of liability; a second payment on account is payable on or by the following 31 July.

This example can best be explained by illustration with figures. Assuming that a balance of £1,000 income tax payable toward the 2001–02 tax year has arisen on submission of the 2002 tax return you will be required to make the following payments:

	£
2001–02 balance	1000
2002–03 first payment on account	500
Total payable 31 January 2003	1500
2002–03 second payment on account	500
Total payable 31 July 2003	500

The payments on account will be held pending receipt of the 2003 tax return, and offset against any ensuing liability, with any outstanding liability being again due for payment on 31 January 2004 along with the next payment on account.

Your attention is drawn to the potential trap that can occur when you have either fresh sources of income not taxed at source arising in a tax year, or rising partnership profits. In such cases the liability payable in the following January is disproportionately greater, due to the requirement to not only settle the balance of the prior-year liability not covered by the preceding payments on account but also, to pay increased payments on account for the current tax year. This can be compounded when completion of the tax return is left to the last minute without prior consideration of an individual's potential liability.

If an individual partner's share of profit is expected to decrease or, alternatively, their aggregate taxable income falls, and as a result the anticipated balance of income tax payable is lower that the previous year, a taxpayer may complete and submit Inland Revenue Form SA303 (*Claim to reduce payments on account*) officially notifying the Revenue of their intention to make reduced interim payments.

Tax planning

It almost goes without saying that firstly you should ensure that you do not pay more tax than is equitable in your first years as an equity partner. If the partnership's profits are not rising you should consider very carefully your reasons for joining the firm at all. After all, you are giving up your rights as an employee.

You should ensure that you make the maximum use of all tax reliefs to which you may be entitled. Some of these are set out below. While you will usually have to prove the exact amount of expenditure claimed, it is possible to claim some estimated expenditure or allowances to cover incidental expenses, such as for the use of your private motor vehicle on behalf of your business. The amount of which will depend on your actual business mileage (not including travel to and from work) as a proportion of your overall mileage. The Revenue will usually require you to keep records of your mileage and you must therefore be able to prove your claim for the relief in full if called upon to do so.

Allowances available

Interest on loans

Probably the most important item(s) to claim will be interest on loans (other than overdrafts, which do not qualify) which you take out to provide capital for the partnership. Tax relief for the interest arising on such loans will be given at your highest marginal rate.

Interest on loans taken out to purchase goodwill of the partnership, or to acquire property or equipment for partnership use may also qualify. If you are not a full equity partner, you should seek advice from your taxation adviser to ensure relief will be available to you. You should also seek advice if you intend to charge the partnership for the use of that asset.

The same relief may be available if you are purchasing an interest in an incorporated practice (subject to conditions upon which you should take advice), although so far these are rare.

Retirement provisions

There are a number of contracts available so far as pensions are concerned, from retirement annuities contracts, replaced from 1 July 1988 by personal pension plans, to the recently introduced stakeholder pensions. You will probably need to seek the advice of your firm's tax adviser to ascertain the precise amount of contribution available to you for this purpose. Increasing percentages are available to those passing through specific age thresholds.

It should be noted that with effect from 6 April 2001 basic rate relief for contributions to personal and stakeholder pensions is given at source. Additional higher rate relief is claimed by way of a deduction when your year-end income tax liability is calculated.

Life cover

You should also consider what provision you have made for the payment of a lump sum on death to protect your family; such a provision is often required by the partnership agreement.

Contributions to a qualifying policy for such a large sum may attract tax relief, subject to a limit of five per cent of net relevant earnings. Those contributions are taken into account in determining the overall limit of pension contributions.

Personal expenses

You should pay special attention to see that personal expenses incurred on behalf of the firm are claimed for tax purposes. Other than car expenses you may also be able to claim for stationery, certain subscriptions, business calls on your home or mobile telephone and indeed use of your home for business purposes. You should be careful with this last item, however, because if you use a particular room of your home as an office you may restrict the relief for capital gains tax when you come to sell your house.

If you are claiming relief for use of a private asset such as your car for the benefit of the business, you should ensure that the relief claimed is for your benefit and not for the firm as a whole.

Salaries for partners' spouses

Some firms pay salaries to partners' spouses which are allowed as an expense for tax purposes in the firm's accounts, and enable the spouse to use up his or her personal allowance. Any balance may be taxed at basic rate thus avoiding the charge to higher tax if the money were received by the partner instead.

Strictly, for the partnership to obtain a deduction for tax purposes, such payments should be clearly linked to services provided by the spouse, and represent a reasonable level of remuneration for those services.

Trading expenses

The normal commercial expenses paid by any firm such as staff salaries and rent and rates are, of course, generally fully deductible and need no emphasis.

Proper reserve for taxation

While the firm has no liability to income tax, the use of tax reserves is advisable. It is the individual partner's responsibility to ensure that he or she keeps back sufficient money to meet his or her share of the tax burden. A benefit to the firm of creating tax reserves is that of providing short-term working capital for the firm. Each firm has their own method of providing for the partners' tax liabilities. The safest method is to reserve for all future taxes payable by reference to profits earned so far. Ideally you should settle with the firm's accountant the basis for setting aside these reserves. You should be aware of what the effect is likely to be when a partner leaves the firm, and ensure that provision for this is set out fully in your partnership agreement.

It is normal to give full credit to each partner for such part of his or her personal allowances and deductions as will be granted in practice against his or her share of the firm's assessment. Inevitably this cannot be done exactly when making provisions.

A problem of reserving for all future liability is that it will affect your own personal cash flow either because your drawings are insufficient or your borrowing excessive, or quite possibly both.

The whole situation of reserves has become much simpler since the introduction of the 'current year' basis of taxation; prior to this the whole consideration process was much more complicated.

Tax treatment as a salaried partner

Although a salaried partner is equally responsible to the outside world for the firm's debts (including tax) you are likely to be taxed as an employee on Schedule E. Exceptionally, however, you will be taxed as an equity partner on Schedule D, particularly if the partnership deed provides something along the lines that you are entitled to such share of the profits as equals £x. The advantage is that under the rules for Schedule D in order to claim allowable expenditure against tax you need only show that this was incurred wholly and exclusively for the purpose of the business and you do not have to overcome the additional hurdle of an employee in showing that it was incurred wholly, exclusively and necessarily.

As an employee taxed under Schedule E you will be taxed under the PAYE scheme with tax deducted at source from your pay.

The national insurance position

If you are a salaried partner treated as an employee both you and the firm will pay Class 1 contributions.

As an equity partner you are treated as self-employed so you will pay Class 2 contributions which are £2.00 per week for the 2002–03 year (assuming earnings are more than £4,615 per annum) and Class 4 contributions of seven per cent on assessable profits between £4,615 and £30,420 per annum, again for the 2002–03 year.

Other tax implications

Capital gains tax

Unlike partnership income, partnership gains and losses are apportioned between, and assessed on, individual partners. Liability is not joint and several. Because of the limited guidance on partnership capital gains given by statute, capital gains tax liability is determined by reference to a Revenue statement of practice. This area is very complex and generally advice should be sought from your taxation adviser. Your introduction as a partner will generally change the ratios in which the firm's asset surpluses are shared. Each of the existing partners' shares will go down to correspond with the share which you are acquiring. Each existing partner therefore makes a part disposal of their share. The existing partner will only incur capital gains tax liability if they make a chargeable gain. This can happen in a variety of ways. For example, if there has been an upward revaluation of the firm's assets in the balance sheet since they acquired their respective shares, or if they receive cash or other consideration either through or outside the accounts which is greater than their respective base values, or if the transfer of shares between the existing partners and you is not at arm's length and the market value of the firm's assets is in excess of the sum which you are paying to join the firm. This last possibility may become more likely if you are related to any of the existing partners.

The fact that you are introducing capital to the firm does not necessarily cause the others to pay capital gains tax; it is either the alteration in asset surplus sharing ratios or payment outside the partnership which raises the possibility of a charge.

If you do not pay for your interest in the partnership, this may amount to a gift resulting in liability unless the existing partners could show that there was no intention to confer a gift and that this was a bona fide commercial transaction. This might be in the form of mutual covenants in the partnership deed. Although hold-over relief for capital gains on gifts was severely curtailed by the Finance Act 1989 it is still available on gifts of business assets.

All the other usual reliefs apply. Generally speaking, any chargeable gains or allowable losses accruing from 31 March 1982 are brought into charge. Since 6 April 1990 husbands and wives each have separate annual exemptions. The annual exemption for 2002–03 is £7,700. From 6 April 1991 unincorporated traders have been able to set trading losses against capital gains arising on both personal and business assets, ICTA, s.380 as extended by FA1991, s.72, although if the firm has been losing money you should be questioning why you are joining it.

For the retiring partner aged at least 50 (or who is retiring on grounds of ill health before that age) retirement relief may be available. Since 1999 this particular relief has been reduced and will be withdrawn entirely at the end of the 2003–04 tax year. Business Asset Taper relief is also available for business assets held for at least two years. It should be noted that indexation is available to existing partners who joined the partnership prior to 17 March 1998 until April 1998, at which point this relief was frozen and taper relief was introduced. The effective tax rate for higher rate taxpayers realising gains on business assets held for more than two years is 10 per cent, based on the fact that only 25 per cent of the gain will remain in charge after application of taper relief and before any allowable annual exemption.

Inheritance tax

Inheritance tax is charged only on death or chargeable lifetime transfers. Briefly, an outright gift without reservation will normally be a potentially exempt transfer. Inheritance tax would normally only arise if the donor dies within seven years of the gift. Again you can counter any inference of gift by showing that there is an arm's length transaction without gratuitous intent. In practice this should not be a major problem, except where relations are involved in the transfer. A clause in the partnership agreement providing for the automatic accrual of any partner's share or giving an option to purchase it at 'undervalue' will mean that his or her share is worth less than it would have been without such a restriction. This may be overcome by mutual covenants to be a partner on the agreed terms, to work full time in the business and to provide each other with pension arrangements compensating for the diminution in the value of the share.

If a capital payment is to be made for a partnership share on the premature death of a partner, rather than an accrual clause, it may be better to have an option clause, under which the personal representatives of the deceased partner have the option to sell, and the surviving partners have an option to buy, to avoid a number of technical arguments which have been raised over the applicability of business property relief. In this way there is a binding contract for sale before the deceased's death. Otherwise the sale of the deceased partner's share will be by the personal representatives who do not qualify for the relief.

Stamp duty

A partnership agreement will not normally be chargeable to stamp duty since in most cases it will not amount to a conveyance or transfer on sale. However, you should not overlook stamp duty as it may be chargeable where the agreement involves a conveyance, or transfer on sale of property for cash, or other consideration such as the assumption of existing liabilities. If you are in any doubt you should present the agreement for adjudication.

The contribution of capital, credited to the new partner's capital account, is not liable for stamp duty (unless perhaps this coincides with the simultaneous reduction in share of another partner and a withdrawal of capital by that partner).

Any document transferring an interest in the partnership in return for consideration may attract *ad valorem* duty on adjudication.

The position regarding stamp duty is undergoing reform; the proposed changes may be implemented at the end of 2003.

VAT considerations

You will need to check that the firm has submitted its returns both correctly and promptly and paid all value added tax by the due dates, otherwise there may be a liability to penalties. Where a return is made late, or tax is paid late in relation to two prescribed tax periods both ending within a period of one year, the Customs and Excise may serve notice of a surcharge period, normally the year following the end of the second default return. If any return or payment in the surcharge period is made late there will be an automatic surcharge of two per cent of the tax due subject to a minimum of £30 in the first period, rising to a maximum of 15 per cent in subsequent periods. In addition to the above, penalties can be imposed for misdeclarations, repeated misdeclarations or neglect under VATA 1994, s.63 and s.64. You will therefore want to be assured that the firm's VAT records and returns are as they should be and the tax paid up to date.

PAYE considerations

As in the case of VAT you should check that the firm's PAYE procedures are in good order. Stringent penalties are now in force for errors such as incorrect completion of Form P11D (the form for declaration of benefits in kind paid to employees earning more than £8,500 per annum); the penalty may be as much as £3,000 for each Form P11D. This may be a cause for concern, for example, where cars are supplied to salaried partners who are not regarded by the firm as employees – has the firm taken proper advice? Should PAYE have been deducted?

The requirement to notify commencement to trade

The Taxes Management Act 1970, s.7(1) requires that you notify chargeability within six months of the end of a tax year. The Inland Revenue National Insurance Contribution Office (NICO), which deals with the collection of Class 2 national insurance contributions, requires notification of commencement to trade within three months of the end of the month in which self-employment starts. NICO will impose penalties for late notification. Notification of commencement to trade to the Revenue can be achieved through the completion and submission of Inland Revenue form CWF1 *Starting up in business.* This form can be obtained from the Revenue website or from inside their booklet *Thinking of working for yourself?* (ref. P/SE/1 available from local tax offices).

Conclusion

As we said at the start of this chapter, partnership taxation is a complex subject, with tax law and practice changing rapidly. If you are ever in any doubt you should take advice from a professional adviser.

Capital

Ways to capitalise the partnership

It is important to differentiate between the concept of buying a share in a partnership and the capital structure of the partnership. When you buy a share you are making the individuals selling that share richer. Money does not, however, go into the partnership. This chapter deals with the financing of the business of the firm and how you will have to contribute to those finances.

A capital contribution to the firm will generally go towards fixed assets and working capital. Fixed assets represent those costly items that are often taken for granted – premises, library, computer and telephone systems. Working capital represents the 'float' in the firm's bank balance. While expenses regularly need to be paid, receipts from clients are notoriously irregular.

Each business is different and its capital requirements will be different. It is also true that a firm can arrange its capital structure equally well in several different ways. This is largely a matter of culture and choice, what really counts is whether there is sufficient cash to pay for the things that are needed in the business.

As an incoming partner you should assess your liability both on a personal level (how much am I being asked to subscribe as a capital input?) and on a 'corporate' level (what is the extent of the firm's borrowing as a whole for which I will be jointly and severally liable?). At one extreme, a partnership financed exclusively by personal contributions by partners will have no 'corporate' indebtedness. At the other extreme, partners who do not make any capital contribution individually will be jointly and severally liable for the whole amount of the 'corporate' borrowing. In addition to the simplicity of buying fixed assets outright, there is also the possibility of leasing premises, equipment and cars. When assessing the overall picture of a firm, these liabilities will need to be taken into account.

There is no 'correct' way of financing the partnership. It is quite usual to have an even split between personal stakes and joint and several liability, with some key equipment being financed through leasing agreements.

Having a large personal stake in a firm can promote a sense of togetherness and confidence, which a partnership needs to be successful. You should be aware of the overall relationship between borrowing and profits – whether the borrowing is personal or 'corporate'. When times are good and fee income supports a relatively high level of gearing, there is less cause for concern. If fee income diminishes then it will be increasingly difficult to service the debt.

Consider the cash flow of the partnership

The underlying principle of any business is to minimise operating costs and maximise income. If there is a significant delay in turning work in progress into cash in hand this will increase the need for working capital. An increase in turnover will in the short term make things worse rather than better. Positive cash flow is what the business will be aiming to achieve.

As an incoming partner you will need to discuss this from the accounting information available. If a firm does not produce good accounting material then it may already be in trouble or be losing money in ways that are avoidable. In either case the firm will not know because it has not produced the right accounts. It will become apparent, when dealing with such a firm, that although they may be presenting you with all the information at their disposal, the picture is nevertheless incomplete. It is vital that you should find out what the real picture is in advance of making a commitment rather than sharing in their distress at a later stage.

Almost without exception, all firms are now computerised so it should therefore be possible to actively keep up to date with management information. Not only should your prospective partners produce this information for themselves but you should also check that they act upon it. Active management systems within the partnership are of vital significance to its future.

You should treat the opportunity of joining a partnership in the same way as any business opportunity. Although the offer to join a partnership may be flattering, it is important to obtain a full picture of the business in which you are being invited to invest. You may expect complete openness from your prospective partners but you should check that both you and they have all the information you require and then obtain independent financial and legal advice before committing yourself.

Ensure regular monitoring of work in progress and credit control

The raw information for deciding whether a partnership cash flow is healthy will be provided by the systems which monitor work in progress and credit control. You should be extremely careful if a firm cannot produce management accounts up to the end of the preceding month. If those systems are not in place then there will be some doubt as to the strength of its financial control. It used to be the case that partnerships either failed to manage their practices as a business at all, or if they did, then they tended to do so very efficiently. Because of the changes which have taken place in the level and scope of the activity of many firms in the last few years, this is no longer the case. Be aware of the fact that even if time recording is computer-based this does not mean that it is actively managed and converted into cash at the bank as quickly as it should be.

If you are an existing employee of the business it is all the more important for you to seek independent advice on this sort of question. It is sometimes difficult to question the business acumen and management expertise of those by whom you have been trained. Having had your expectations formed by those who are presiding over the business you may not be best placed to form an independent view (see Chapter 9).

Borrowing capital

Introduction

First of all, let us consider the purpose of the borrowing. There are still cases of potential partners being asked to purchase their share of the partnership. If the firm owns freehold property, then there might be validity in the request, but if you are merely being asked to purchase your share of goodwill, then think very carefully. Many years ago, senior partners were accustomed to selling shares of goodwill to incoming partners, as this was the only basis on which they could earn a capital fund, out of which they could have a pension. The government changed that in the late 1950s and now partners will be providing their own pensions out of earnings. With that justification gone, ask very carefully what you are buying.

If you have worked in the firm and helped build up the goodwill, it is normally unconscionable to expect you to pay for your share. Any money that you pay will go into the pockets of other partners, whether outgoing or continuing, and you must ask yourself what chance you have of recovering all or any of that payment from future incoming partners. If the answer is fairly negative, then perhaps you should decline with thanks. The more normal request is to be asked to make a contribution to the working capital of the partnership by way of a loan. If the firm prospers, you should get your money back. It is not possible to be sure one way or the other, so the making of a loan to the partnership must always be treated as something of a gamble. You should know a lot about the past history of the firm, as well as its likely short-term future prospects, which will help you in your judgement (see Chapters 1–4). Such information will also assist a borrower in deciding whether or not to help you and, if so, on what terms.

Ensure your proposed capital contribution is in proportion to your partnership share

There are situations where an incoming partner is expected to make a disproportionate contribution to the working capital of the firm. Any such demands should be fiercely resisted.

It is impossible to give an exact figure as to how much partners are expected to contribute by way of capital to the running of the firm, and hence how much your proportionate contribution should be. There are some surprising variations. Some of the largest and best established firms have relatively low capital requirements while other smaller firms seem to be much more capital hungry. You will have made yourself familiar with the accounts of the firm before you agree partnership terms (see Chapter 10). This will give you an idea of what was required historically, although circumstances and requirements may change, based partly on the demands of the firm's bank, and planned future expenditure of a capital nature. As to the latter, it can often be funded on leasing or similar terms, but with the ever increasing demands for better information technology, law firms are becoming more capital intensive institutions and partners may be expected to contribute more.

It is highly unlikely that you will be able to fund your capital requirements out of your own resources without borrowing. One advantage of this type of borrowing is that it is tax effective, as the interest is an allowable expense. Capital repayment is not.

Negotiating

You should certainly contact the firm's bank, to ascertain whether they are prepared to lend your capital requirements, and, if so, on what terms. If there is a considerable history of the bank lending to new partners, you may be surprised how beneficial the terms are, but it is important that you do your comparison shopping as well.

Your own bank will view you, as a rising young professional, as someone whom they want to hold as a customer on a long-term basis. Once again, the rates may be quite beneficial. You are obviously looking at medium- to long-term borrowing, anything from 15 to 25 years or more. If you personally bank with the firm's bank, then still look elsewhere.

Always remember that the bank's first offer may not be its last. For example, you may be asked for security, but if you demur, that requirement may be waived if the bank is really keen to have or hold onto your business. Ideally, the strength of the firm that you are joining and your future earning power as a partner in it, is sufficient security for the lender. Try to resist a charge on your home, especially if it is jointly owned, as there will be the complications of getting the consent of your spouse or partner to the security.

If you are borrowing from the firm's bank and giving security, read the small print very carefully. You may well find that you have mistakenly charged your home to secure not merely your personal loan but all the firm's borrowings to fund your partnership capital requirements.

Banks often apply add-on services, which earn them money. If the bank requires you to take on new life cover through the bank's agency and you already have enough, ask for it to be substituted as you have no need for more. Strictly speaking, your pension policies are not a valid form of security. Although the bank may want to hold them in the hope they may be able to grab the tax free lump sum when you reach retirement age, if there is no other obvious way of them being repaid.

You need to consider how you are going to repay the capital borrowed. The usual terms do not provide for capital repayment during the course of the loan, but interest payments only. Ideally, when you come to retire, the firm will be in a good financial position and well able to repay. Once again, it is not possible to predict future circumstances, so do consider less optimistic possibilities.

You must also consider the new partnership terms offered to you, in relation to your net annual borrowing costs. If, for example, you are currently earning £50,000 p.a. as a salaried partner and your drawings are to be about the same level as an equity partner, you may find your taxed take-home pay much diminished, if you have to service a partnership loan of £100,000. Remember, as an equity partner you should aim to be better off than you were before, and certainly not prejudiced in the pocket by the change in status.

Do remember that banks need to lend money, so negotiate robustly on your own behalf. If the firm is taking on a number of partners simultaneously, you may be better off doing a group deal as your bargaining power will be that much greater.

Lending rates should be favourable on this type of loan. One or two per cent over base rate is normal. An offer at a higher rate should make you ask questions perhaps about the firm that you are proposing to join. If the firm is not already a customer of the bank, expect to be asked to produce copies of the accounts. Remember, just as you are interested in having enough money to service the loan and still maintain a decent standard of living, so will your proposed lender be concerned.

If you do not like the idea of taking on substantial borrowing, ask your future partners whether you can pay for your capital requirements out of future income. There are still some firms who will be prepared to accept that proposition in whole or in part, but once again you want to make sure that you are left with enough net take home income after servicing the instalment payments. As law firms become more capital hungry, this option is becoming available less often.

The bank is highly likely to ask for an advance fee as part of its terms. Once again, try and reduce this by negotiation, if not eliminate it, but, if you have to pay it, factor it into the overall charges, to ascertain the true rate of interest you have to pay. It is a sad fact of life that banks are in business to make a profit and, unless you are the chairman's son or daughter, you are likely to end up paying commercial terms.

You also need to consider the flexibility of the borrowing arrangement. After all your circumstances may change for the better, in which case you do not want to be penalised for early repayment. The likelihood in reality is that you may want to extend the borrowing term until you reach retirement. Also consider with the bank the prospect of adding onto the loan, if you are asked to increase your partnership share with a commensurate increase in the partnership capital. The bank may not be willing to commit itself in detail, but an indication at the initial stage may be helpful.

Conclusion

Be aware of potential pitfalls if you fail to act with caution and do not insist on adequate information.

CASE STUDY   **A cautionary tale from a partnership solicitor**

I recently acted for an equity partner before the Solicitors' Disciplinary Tribunal. He was there with his senior equity partners. The latter had broken most of the Solicitors' Accounts Rules in their efforts to keep a failing firm afloat. He had accepted an invitation to join the equity with no increase in terms merely so that the partnership could make further borrowings based on his signature on the loan note.

They were all struck off, while he retained his practising certificate, but at the cost of a fine, as he had to plead guilty to conduct unbefitting a solicitor even though he knew nothing about the malpractices of his partners. The Tribunal considered that he, along with any other equity partner, ought to have known.

This is of course an extreme case, but do examine your future partners' motives, as to why they want you to become an equity partner – they may not always be to our advantage.

Pensions and personal insurance

Introduction

Pension legislation and planning is a complicated area and it is worth taking independent financial advice. We would recommend that you talk to your existing adviser. If you do not already have an adviser think about appointing one.

Key times to review your situation

It is easy to spend all the hours in the day striving to do your best for your clients, but it is important not to lose focus on your own situation and ensure that you are doing the best for yourself and more importantly for your family. There are three main situations when a detailed review of personal finance should be made by a lawyer:

1. When your personal situation changes (move house, have children, etc.).

2. When you move from being employed to being self-employed (i.e. promotion to partner, or change of direction to becoming a barrister).

3. When you move between law firms as an employee.

Typical inclusions in solicitor firms benefits packages

Solicitor firms often have good benefits packages on top of the salaries that are paid to employees. These may include the following:

- a pension plan;
- insurance;
- income protection; and
- private medical insurance.

You should make sure that you have a good understanding of the benefits you do have because these can form a significant part of your remuneration. This is an area that should be fully appreciated when negotiating a new salary package, moving to another law firm or being promoted to partner. It is a good time to seek independent financial advice. These are all areas that may also be given consideration by a partner who does not have the luxury of a company to provide a safety net.

Main issues in planning for retirement

Pensions and insurance are often last on a list of things for lawyers to get done, because they do not have an immediate impact. They are however vitally important.

There are many ways that individuals can plan for their retirement and all have a part to play in personal financial planning. Planning for retirement is all about investing for the future. There are broadly four main asset classes, other than leaving your money in cash, in which individuals can invest:

- the stock market;
- commercial property;
- residential property; and
- government and corporate bonds.

Typically when individuals talk about planning for retirement they think of pensions. There are good reasons for this, but it is well to remember that pensions, individual savings accounts (ISAs) and unit trusts are just ways in which shares, property or bonds can be held. Whether the investment will do well or poorly will depend on the underlying investments you make, and not on whether it was in a pension or an ISA. It is important to have a diversified and balanced approach to this area of planning in order to minimise risk.

Key pension rules

This is not an exhaustive list. It merely covers some of the key points.

How much can I put into my pension?

- This will depend upon the type of pension you have in force. You should note that it may not be possible to contribute to more than one type of pension and this is an area of financial planning where independent advice is very important because the legislation is complicated.
- Please note that for a stakeholder pension plan (i.e. personal pension plan) it is possible to make up to £3,600 gross contributions each tax year without having any net relevant earnings. However, in general, the contributions you can make are linked to age and your net relevant earnings as shown in Table 14.1.

Table 14.1 Pension contribution levels

| Age at the beginning | Max. % of net relevant earnings | | |
of tax year (6 April)	Personal pension	Retirement annuity	Occupational scheme
35 or less	17.5	17.5	15
36–45	20	17.5	15
46–50	25	17.5	15
51–55	30	20	15
56–60	35	22.5	15
61–74	40	27.5	15

- You should check with the firm's accountant the precise amount of relief available to you.
- If you make any personal pension or occupational scheme contributions there is a limit on net relevant earnings (not only for personal pensions but normally also for occupational schemes) of £97,200 for the year commencing 6 April 2002. Retirement annuity contracts have no such limits.

When can I use prior year earnings to make a pension contribution?

- For an occupational scheme this is not possible.
- For a retirement annuity you may use the last six years' earnings to make a contribution in the current tax year.
- For a personal pension (including stakeholder) you may use the previous year's earnings to make a current contribution.
- For a personal pension plan (including stakeholder plan) you can base the contribution you make in the current tax year on an earlier year's salary level. This does not mean that you are using these earnings, simply that you can use a certain salary as the basis of making a contribution for the following five tax years.

When can I take benefits?

- For a personal pension benefits may be taken between the ages of 50 and 75.
- For retirement annuity contracts benefits may be taken between the ages of 60 and 75.
- For occupational schemes please refer to the scheme booklet.

What tax free lump sum will I receive on retirement?

- Under personal pensions you can choose to receive at retirement a maximum of 25 per cent of the pension fund as a tax free lump sum.
- Under retirement annuity contracts the maximum tax free lump sum is equal to three times the annuity you can take from the remainder of the fund.
- Under occupational pension plans this will depend on the scheme rules. The maximum allowable is normally 1.5 times the earnings cap, which is currently £97,200.

Benefits of pensions

Pensions have significant advantages over holding assets directly in your own name and this is why they can be attractive to lawyers:

- You receive tax relief on the contributions you make into the plans. This can be up to 40 per cent of the amount you invest for higher rate taxpayers. In other words for making a contribution of £60, the government will put in £40, making an instant return of 66 per cent on your initial investment.
- Investments held within a pension plan usually fall outside your estate for inheritance tax purposes. This can be a significant advantage for families in the event of the death of the policyholder before retirement. Inheritance tax is paid at 40 per cent on estates over £250,000 and so the net benefit of having assets in a pension can be significant.
- The investment funds build up within the pension fund free of further tax.
- It is possible to invest in shares, government and corporate bonds and commercial property via pensions. The latter is usually done by self-employed individuals through the use of a Self Invested Personal Pension (SIPP) plan.
- New stakeholder pension plans are the lowest charged investment contracts on the market, with no initial charges and annual management charges of one per cent or less. This can make them more attractive than non-pension products.

Before investing in pensions you should appreciate that under current legislation:

- your investment will not be accessible until you are 50 (precise age dependent on pension scheme):
- at the age of 75 you are required to purchase an annuity (an income stream for life) using much of your investment.

To some extent these considerations may offset the advantages of pensions but they should still remain a part of retirement planning for most people.

Benefits of ISAs

It is possible to invest £7,000 per tax year into a Maxi ISA each year (assuming you have not opened a Mini ISA in the same tax year). The benefits of an ISA are that the fund will grow without the payment of further taxes. In this way they are similar to pensions. The benefits of an ISA over a pension are that:

- 100 per cent of the investment fund can be taken as a tax free lump sum;
- If you take an income from an ISA there is no income tax to pay, as opposed to a pension where an annuity will be chargeable at your marginal rate of tax which, under current legislation, could be up to 40 per cent.

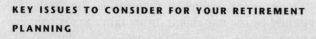

KEY ISSUES TO CONSIDER FOR YOUR RETIREMENT PLANNING

➤ Make the most of company pension scheme arrangements, while you are eligible as an employee.

➤ Upon promotion from employee to partner you will no longer be eligible for the company pension scheme, whether it be a group personal pension plan or an occupational scheme. This means that you will have to make private pension provision.

➤ Consider transferring existing pension plans into the new lower charge stakeholder schemes. (This should be discussed with an independent financial adviser.)

➤ Consider using the new lower charge stakeholder pension plans for future private contributions (you may not be able to do so if you have a company pension scheme and earn in excess of £30,000).

➤ Make use of Individual Savings Accounts (ISAs) and other investment vehicles such as Open Ended Investment Companies (OEICs) and unit trusts.

➤ Make contributions into a stakeholder plan for your spouse (it is possible to contribute up to £3,600 per year gross even if your spouse does not work).

Main issues with regard to insurance

Insurance premiums are often viewed as money wasted. Statistics show however, that it makes good sense to provide for yourself and your family in case the future does not turn out as you expect. An independent financial adviser would be happy to assist you with the type and level of cover you should consider.

The basic types of insurance are:

- life assurance;
- income protection;
- critical illness insurance

Life assurance

- This pays out on the death of the life assured, usually this is the policyholder.
- These plans should normally be written in trust because as such they are paid direct to the trustees (usually the beneficiaries) without having to wait for probate to be completed and without having to pay any inheritance tax.
- Life assurance is generally only needed where the life assured has financial dependants, typically these would be a spouse and children. If the life assured is not in this position he or she might be better advised to insure other areas of his or her life first.

Income protection

This pays out an income replacement in the event that you cannot work due to illness. It is sensible to take out this cover because lawyers' financial commitments are often high and the state does not provide any material level of help. The maximum level of benefit which is available is three-quarters of normal earnings, less the single person's state Invalidity Benefit.

The benefit will normally become payable after an initial deferment of 13 or 26 weeks (although deferred periods of four, eight, 13, 26, 52 and 104 weeks can be arranged) and will continue throughout the incapacity or until your chosen retirement date. You should ensure that there is provision for the benefits payable to be increased in line with increases in the cost of living.

Critical illness insurance

This pays out a lump sum upon the diagnosis of a critical illness. We recommend this as a minimum to repay your mortgage. It is not linked to your ability to work, but is designed to take the pressure off earning at a time where your health may make work less desirable.

Critical illnesses are now being detected earlier, with the result that one major insurance company has reduced the terms of its cover. Others may follow suit. Where insurance plans are reviewable this could lead to premium increases and/or reductions in cover. It is recommended that policyholders review their critical illness plans and consider changing to guaranteed terms or premiums where they are available.

A sensible level of cover for life assurance

The general rule of thumb is that a lump sum pay out can be used to provide an income of five per cent. Therefore if you want to provide an income for your family of £10,000, you will need to have life cover of £200,000. You should also aim to repay any outstanding loans or mortgage.

If you have death in service cover through work this may meet some of this need. However, it is as well to remember that this kind of insurance is only paid while you remain in service of the company. If you move company or are promoted to partner then the cover will cease and you will need to provide your own cover. The problem with waiting for this time to come is that you may have health problems by this stage and not be insurable. It is therefore often advisable to ignore death in service cover when considering the minimum life assurance you need to cover your dependants.

The basic form of life assurance is term cover. This is usually the most appropriate form of cover to obtain. It is a simple contract with no investment element that provides cover for a fixed cost per month, guaranteed over the term of the contract.

Term assurance plans are just one of the options. Cost and product benefits can be gained by going through an adviser intermediary. If you are thinking of obtaining critical illness insurance as well, the life cover can often be included on top of this for free.

It is important to review your financial planning regularly to take account of changing personal circumstances and fluctuations in the investment and insurance markets.

Partnership insurance considerations

A partnership is a business designed to trade for profit. Its profitability depends upon its personnel and the key personnel are generally the partners. For the partnership to survive, its income must exceed its outgoings, and it is therefore crucial that no undue calls for money be made upon the partnership, either by the individuals that make it up or by others.

In order to survive financially the partnership must at all times be able to buy out partners who wish to leave and to cope should the earnings of any of the partners discontinue due to death, departure or disability. In addition, the partnership must ensure that claims made against it by claimants in civil proceedings will be covered by professional indemnity insurance.

You may well find, depending upon the nature of the practice in question, that some, or all, of the above will have been considered by the present partners and suitable arrangements will be in place.

You must establish how far these arrangements go. For instance, is provision for illness a partnership responsibility, or alternatively is it the individual responsibility of the partners? If the partnership covers this, for how long, for how much and to whom is the benefit payable? Is further individual cover necessary? You should also consider the point at which on illness the partners may require you to leave the firm, when do drawings cease and when does the obligation to buy out the ill partner's share arise? Your personal arrangements should be tailored to fit as closely as possible with the partnership's arrangements.

KEY POINTS TO CONSIDER WITH REGARD TO INSURANCE

➤ Life insurance, income protection and critical illness insurance can all be important depending upon your own situation.

➤ Simple life insurance contracts are rate driven i.e. purely assessed on cost (and the financial strength of the insurance company concerned). It is important to consider the *terms* of critical illness and income protection plans alongside *costs* when considering which insurance company to use, because these policies have exclusions which do vary from company to company.

➤ Insurance cover may be included within employee benefits packages and it is unlikely that these will extend to partners (for example, death in service cover will end). It is important to take this into consideration when planning for the future. It may be sensible to ignore company benefits in your planning with regard to life and critical illness cover and take out policies immediately while you are still a good risk for an insurance company from a health perspective.

15

Indemnity insurance

Principals (which includes partners and sole principals) in private practice in England and Wales are obliged by the Solicitors' Indemnity Insurance Rules from year to year to have compulsory indemnity insurance of £1 million for any one claim. This must indemnify against civil liability arising from private legal practice, subject to certain specified exclusions (which include wrongful dismissal, trading debts, death and injury). Cover against defamation, breach of undertakings, and loss of paperwork is included, and the cover extends to all employees of the practice.

Until 31 August 2000 indemnity could only be obtained from the Solicitors' Indemnity Fund (SIF) which was a mutual fund to which all principals in private practice had to contribute. From 1 September 2000, SIF ceased to provide this compulsory indemnity, and compulsory indemnity insurance can now be obtained from a number of qualifying insurers on the open market. Each qualifying insurer is required to enter into an agreement with the Law Society to guarantee a certain level of protection or cover for both firms and their clients. The indemnity insurance offered by qualifying insurers must comply with certain minimum terms and conditions that are appended to the Solicitors' Indemnity Insurance Rules.

The cover afforded by such qualifying insurance operates on a 'claims made' basis rather than on an 'occurrence' basis. This means that the responsibility for handling a claim lies with the qualifying insurer at the time the claim is made, rather than with the insurer on cover at the time the alleged negligent act took place. Principals will want to be familiar with the terms of their firm's particular indemnity insurance policy and, in particular, be aware of the time limits and conditions attaching to the notification of claims, or circumstances which may give rise to a claim which also must be notified to a qualifying insurer.

It is important to note that no distinction is made between equity and salaried partners, both of which will be held to be jointly and severally liable for claims arising during their period of partnership.

SIF still exists to collect the shortfall contribution, to deal with claims already notified to it prior to 1 September 2000, and to provide run-off cover where a principal retired before 1 September 2000 with no successor practice. From 1 September 2002 the Solicitors' Indemnity Rules 2002 apply to the continued existence of SIF.

Complicated provisions exist defining when a firm may, as a matter of contract, restrict its liability to clients. However, this can never be below the level of the £1 million compulsory cover. For further information on this see principle 12.11 in *The Guide to the Professional Conduct of Solicitors 1999*, published by the Law Society, and at **www.guide-on-line.lawsociety.org.uk**.

Needless to say, the cover provided by the compulsory indemnity insurance may not always be sufficient to satisfy potential claims and so a firm may well wish to have further insurance cover in place. The amount of top-up cover required will, of course, depend largely upon the type of work which the practice deals with, both in terms of the sums involved and the degree of risk inherent in the work. Top-up insurance is not subject to the Solicitors' Indemnity Insurance Rules, and firms are free to make whatever arrangements they deem appropriate and not necessarily with a qualifying insurer. Without this top-up cover partners who are equally responsible for the liabilities of a firm might find themselves faced with a large claim and insufficient resources to meet it. This is not only a risk faced by firms dealing with high-value or complex work.

Principals should check whether top-up cover has a fixed limit for the period of indemnity or a limit per claim. If the former, you must be careful during the rest of the year after a claim has been made, as the level of top-up cover may have been reduced and you may wish to take out further cover.

Information about any of the above can be obtained from the Professional Indemnity Department of the Law Society.

Further reading

Armour, D. (2001) *Limited Liability Partnership: the new legislation*, Lexis Nexis Butterworths Tolley.

Banks, R.I. (2002) *Lindley and Banks on Partnership* 18th edn, Sweet & Maxwell.

Blackett-Ord, M. (2002) *Partnership – The modern law of partnership and limited liability partnership*, Lexis Nexis Butterworths Tolley.

Machell, J., Whittaker, J. and Ives, C. (2001) *Limited Liability Partnerships: the new law*, Jordan Publishing.

Morse, G. (2001) *Palmer's Limited Liability Partnership Law*, Sweet & Maxwell.

Sacker, T. (2002) *Practical Partnership Agreements* 2nd edn, Jordan Publishing.

Sapp, J.R. (2002) *Making Partner: A guide for law firm associates* 2nd edn, American Bar Association.

The Smith & Williamson Group (2002) *Professional Partnership Handbook* 4th edn, Lexis Nexis Butterworths Tolley.

Tupman, S. (2000) *Why Lawyers Should Eat Bananas: Inspirational ideas for lawyers wanting more out of life*, Simon Tupman Presentations Pty, Australia.

Young, S. (2001) *Tolley's Limited Liability Partnerships Handbook*, Lexis Nexis Butterworths Tolley.

Useful contacts

Young Solicitors Group (YSG)
Groups Co-ordinator
The Law Society
113 Chancery Lane
Tel: 020 7320 5793
Web: **www.ysg.org**

Law Society

Association of Women Solicitors
The Law Society
113 Chancery Lane
London
WC2A 1PL
Tel: 020 7320 5793

Law Society Recruitment
113 Chancery Lane
Tel: 020 7320 5880
Fax: 020 7583 5561
E-mail: recruitment@lawsociety.org.uk
Web: **www.recruitment.lawsociety.org.uk**

A commercial unit within the Law Society that deals with permanent, locum and paralegal placements.

Practice Advice
The Law Society
113 Chancery Lane
Tel: 0870 606 2522
Fax: 020 7316 5541
E-mail: lib-pas@lawsociety.org.uk

This service is staffed by solicitors working from various information sources including a database of Law Society policy and practice and drawing on the experience of colleagues in other departments of the Law Society. The great majority of telephone enquiries can be answered immediately.

Professional Ethics
Ipsley Court
Berrington Close
Redditch
Worcestershire
B98 0TD
DX: 19114 Redditch
Tel: 0870 606 2577
Web: **www.guide-on-line.lawsociety.org.uk**

They produce a guide called 'Incorporated Practice: LLPs' which can be obtained by telephone or visiting the website.

Professional Indemnity
Ipsley Court
Tel: 01527 504487/88

Registration Department
Ipsley Court
Tel: 0870 606 2555

Services to the Profession
113 Chancery Lane
Tel: 020 7320 5698
Web: **www.sbs.lawsociety.org.uk**

Holds details of specially negotiated insurance and financial schemes for business and personal use.

Solicitors Assistance Scheme (SAS)
Policy Support Executive
The Law Society
113 Chancery Lane
Tel: 020 7320 5795

If solicitors are looking for help with personal or professional issues – including partnership, financial and employment matters – they can call the Solicitors Assistance Scheme in total confidence. The scheme comprises nearly 100 solicitors from all over the country who are willing to lend an understanding ear to a fellow solicitor. The scheme is administered from the Law Society and solicitors can request a leaflet showing members of the scheme, their specialisms and telephone numbers.

Others

Association of Chartered Certified Accountants (ACCA)
29 Lincoln's Inn Fields
London
WC2A 3EE
Tel: 020 7396 7000
Fax: 020 7396 7070
E-mail: info@accaglobal.com
Web: **www.acca.org.uk**

The Association of Chartered Certified Accountants (ACCA) is the largest global professional accountancy body, with nearly 300,000 members and students in 160 countries. The website includes a directory of members and business advisers.

Financial Services Authority
25 The North Colonnade
Canary Wharf
London
E14 5HS
Tel: 0845 606 1234 (consumer helpline)
Web: **www.fsa.gov.uk** (includes consumer help site)

The Financial Services Authority (FSA) is an independent non-governmental body, given statutory powers by the Financial Services and Markets Act 2000. Amongst other objectives, the FSA aims to help people gain the knowledge, aptitude and skills they need to become informed consumers, so that they can manage their financial affairs more effectively.

Freelance Solicitors Group
Natalie Siabkin
5 The Link
West Acton
London
W3 0JW
Tel: 020 8992 3885
Web: **www.users.aol.com/pjmiller00/freelance.html**

The Freelance Solicitors Group was originally founded in September 1993 as the Locum Solicitors Group. It represents the interests of those solicitors in England and Wales who work as solicitor for others on a locum, contract or freelance basis.

LawCare Ltd
PO Box 6
Porthmadog
Gwynedd
LL49 9ZE
Tel: 0800 018 4299 (freephone helpline 9–7.30 weekdays/10–4 weekends)
E-mail: help@lawcare.org.uk
Web: **www.lawcare.org.uk**

Offers a free and confidential helpline and e-mail to discuss health issues and problems which are interfering with, or have the potential to interfere with, work performance and/or family life – and to seek help in resolving the problem in its early stages.

Law Monkeys
Web: **www.lawmonkeys.com**

Law Monkeys is a website run by lawyers for lawyers. It aims to provide a free, reliable and objective discussion forum for all those connected with the legal profession.

Rollonfriday
9 Carmelite Street
London
EC4Y 0DR
Fax: 020 7072 8552
E-mail: info@rollonfriday.com
Web: **www.rollonfriday.com**

A website that provides news, views and gossip on the legal profession – including the top firms' salaries.

Index